Praise for Sweet Adversity

"With her unique gift of bringing people to life through words, Sandra welcomes the reader into her world with wit, wisdom, and a clear appreciation that relationships are the essence of a rich life. This book is a collage of short stories as well as creative nonfiction. Sandra's fiction is a compelling look at topics ranging from genetics to weddings. Her almost true stories celebrate the lives and relationships of Sandra's kinfolk. A true daughter of the South, she shares memories of folks she knew while growing up and living in Alabama and Tennessee, amidst all its cultural complexities and contradictions."
—Lisa Atkinson

"In a professional communicator's fond recollections of growing up, Sandra creates a warm and inviting glimpse of her past, finding adventures of years gone by on the tip of her tongue. Along with sibling rivalry, parental interactions, and unusual encounters, Sandra's dialogue and point of view remain fresh and flow easily on the page as if happening in real time. This is a treasured work highlighting her gift and passion for writing." —Beverly McKenzie

"Sandra Plant is a mentor for all of us aspiring writers in the community-based Joy in Learning program at Westminster Presbyterian Church here in Nashville. She is herself a very accomplished writer, and in this book she 'struts her stuff!'"
—Sarah Wilkinson

"Sandra's memory is as sharp as her sense of humor. Tales of cathead biscuits, summer straw fedoras, and glory-to-God hair will warm your heart and make you giggle."
—*New York Times* bestselling author Jane Lorenzini,
  The Growing Season

SWEET ADVERSITY

A Southern Writer Finds Stories
—and Good—in Everything

Sandra Whitten Plant

Knoxville, Tennessee, USA
crippledbeaglepublishing.com

Photography by iStock: Nancy Anderson
Cover design by: Maria Loysa-Bel Nueve – de los Angeles

Paperback ISBNs 978-1-958533-68-0, 978-1-958533-69-7
Hardcover ISBNs 978-1-958533-70-3, 978-1-958533-71-0
eBook ISBN 978-1-958533-75-8

Library of Congress Control Number: 2024900872

Printed in the United States of America

Sweet are the uses of adversity
Which, like the toad, ugly and venomous,
Wears yet a precious jewel in his head;
And this our life, exempt from public haunt,
Finds tongues in trees, books in the running brooks,
Sermons in stones, and good in everything.

—William Shakespeare
As You like It, Act 2, Scene 1, Lines 12 – 17

To my parents Sadye and Jim Whitten, who always encouraged me.

Sadye Henry Baird Whitten, the author's mother who inspired stories in Sweet Adversity, stands with little Sadye's grandfather Henry. Sadye adored her grandfather but was embarrassed to have a man's name as her middle name.

CONTENTS

Introduction

One afternoon when I was nine years old, I came home from school complaining about a fellow student in my fourth-grade classroom. Neither my fellow student's name nor his or her offense remains in my memory, but the life lesson imparted by my daddy when he heard my unkind remark was stamped into my memory for the rest of my life.

Daddy directed me to a few lines written by William Shakespeare that begin, "Sweet are the uses of adversity." The final line preached the message about "finding good in everything." Daddy made me memorize those lines; every time he heard me find fault in someone I had to quote those lines. Of course, I didn't totally reform from my negative comments about family and friends, but I did think of Shakespeare's message from time to time.

It is my hope as you read these stories that you find that there truly is "good in everything," whether it be human nature, bigotry, war, death, or simply an incident in your life that didn't feel so good at the time. Realization of the "good in everything" may take only a moment or perhaps thirty years, even a lifetime, but the good is always there. —Sandra Whitten Plant, 2024

Sweet Adversity

Mama was giving our cousin Nona a Toni Home Permanent which took a lot of concentration, she said. She told me and Jim Boy to stay in our own yard today. Even though I was only in third grade, Mama wasn't much taller than I was, but she looked a lot bigger when she put her hand on her hip and leaned over almost level with the finger she was shaking in our faces. "If you cross Wilson Road to play with Randy and Emeline," she warned, "I'll whip you with a switch." From past experience, I didn't doubt that she meant what she said. I especially hated the part when she said, "Janis, go find the switch. You're gonna get it." Jim Boy usually got out of a whipping by acting innocent or something. I bet I got ten times more whippings than he did.

Mama shooed us out of the house so she could get started on cousin Nona's permanent. And sure enough, they were out there, Randy and Emeline standing on the other side of Wilson Road hollering at me and Jim Boy to come on over. He's just two years younger than me, but I could see Jim Boy's big eyes watching me so he could copy whatever I did. At first, I yawned and looked away, trying to ignore them. Then I squatted down on our side of the road and picked up an old popsicle stick from the gravel. As I dragged the stick through the black tar that oozed around the gravels on these hot summer days, I pulled up strings of black goo and stuck the mess close to Jim Boy who thought I was going to smear it on him. He whined and fell over on the gravel path beside the road as Randy and Emeline laughed.

"Y'all come on over here," crooned Randy, his dirt-stained toes digging into the vine-like strips of zoysia grass that grew by the side of the road despite the dust and the heat. "Come on, we'll play in the creek."

"We can't do that," I said weakly. "Our mama would kill us." I looked longingly toward the creek where water, putrid from the slaughterhouse just upstream, cut a deep gash through the red clay soil beside Randy and Emeline's house. I was dying to play in the creek, to explore the tunnel-like holes on its banks.

Emeline sneered, "What's keeping you from it, sissy? Your mama don't have to know everything; just don't let little blabbermouth Jim Boy tell everything he knows." Emeline was a beanpole of a girl with bobbed black hair and blue eyes so vivid that I didn't doubt her when she said she could hypnotize a snake.

Jim Boy twisted nervously beside me, pulling on the neck of his yellow T-shirt. A cement truck rumbled by, churning the hot summer air that swirled his golden blond hair for a moment; then it fell back in place.

Then Jim Boy whispered in my ear, "There's Mama looking out the front window." We both took a step back from the edge of Wilson Road to stand in the more neutral gravel sidewalk. Mama nodded her approval and went back to the permanent, probably to put more solution on our cousin Nona's new hairdo.

"Come on, you chickenshit," yelled Randy, his dirty shorts falling well below his navel that looked like the cut-off tail of a pig. I boldly stepped back to the edge of the road. Jim Boy eased beside me after a minute or two, making sure that Mama wasn't looking.

Emeline cut her eyes toward their house. "Shut up, you stupid," she said to Randy with a scowl. Grandma Crouch is in there and she don't put up with none of that dirty talk."

The preacher from Powderly Baptist Church drove by, careful not to run over the children on either side of the street. The tires on his black Pontiac stuck to the melting tar on the road, making sounds like ripping a Band-Aid off a hairy arm as he rolled on down the road. A hood ornament on the preacher's car had arms outstretched like angel wings. I thought it was really nice for the preacher to be riding along with the angel of the Lord leading the way.

All four of us watched together as the preacher stuck his arm out the window to signal a left turn. He slowed his car and turned down the side road toward the slaughterhouse and meat market. Our Uncle Bill and Aunt Annalee lived down that road where Uncle Bill worked in the meat market. Randy displayed his middle finger to the preacher's car as it disappeared down the road. "Climb this," he said with a sneer.

I didn't know what any of this meant, but it looked wonderfully nasty. I would practice this gesture in the dark tonight in the room I shared with Jim Boy. I would mouth the words so Jim Boy wouldn't tell Mama. Then Emeline, with a solemn face, called, "Come on over so we can play a while before the snakes come out again."

"What're you talking about?" I asked.

"Don't you know about the snakes, you big dummy?' Emeline sneered. Randy wiped his nose with his hand, leaving a clean spot in the grime on his face, at least around his nose." Them snakes come out of the holes in the creek bank two times a day. They was out about a hour ago and they won't be back till about…about two o'clock," she said with a glance toward the sun.

"That's right," said Randy. "They was a wrapping around my leg and everything. They was all over that side yard."

"But they won't do nothing now," said Emeline. "They're resting up before they come out again."

That got me to thinking. Our mama said don't cross Wilson Road. She didn't say anything about getting over to Randy and Emeline's some other way. I whispered to Jim Boy. "Why don't we go across the side road and get down in the creek? We can wade and go under the bridge to Randy and Emeline's."

His big blue eyes got bigger and filled with tears. "I don't know, I'm scared of the snakes."

"But you heard Emeline say they're resting now. They won't bother us till two o'clock and we'll be back home by then."

Just to prove that I can never get by with anything, not even a sneaky thought, I gasped as the preacher's car turned the corner and pulled into our driveway. He got out of the car, and to my relief, he didn't come over to me and Jim Boy. He stood by the car door while he pulled on the coat to his suit. I could see the shiny threads glinting in the sun, looking something like a suit of armor I had seen in my grandmother's *National Geographic*. He looked at himself in the side mirror and straightened his gray tie.

He nodded our way as he walked past our mama's patch of red verbena growing beside the house. As he climbed the front steps, he called to us, "How're you children doing this hot day?" I loved the way his gray hair was poufed up in front like a movie star's hair.

I knew our mama would be panicked that the preacher had come by right in the middle of Nona's permanent wave. I could see that frantic look on her face when she opened the screen door. And there behind Mama was Nona, looking embarrassed and sort of bald headed with her hair all twisted on those little plastic rods, maybe a hundred or more. Nona was one of those teenagers who didn't want anybody seeing her with messy hair or anything like that.

You can count on that preacher to catch you when you don't want to be caught, my daddy had said one time. I wondered how even a preacher could stand the putrid smell of that pink stuff that Mama dabbed on each wad of Nona's hair as she wound it around the rods. The smell was worse than rotten eggs and cleaning ammonia at the same time. Then I remembered that preachers are supposed to suffer for the Lord. Maybe he could hold his nose, but the stuff would still make his eyes water. When I saw the shiny suit disappear inside, I knew Mama would be too busy timing the permanent solution and talking to the preacher to keep an eye on me and Jim Boy. Here's our chance!

I took Jim Boy's hand and we crossed the side road, walked through the weeds, then slid down the creek bank. Minnie Joyce Green's little brown and white pony was tied to a stake beside the creek bank where he lifted his head to watch. The water in the creek was warm. My bare feet rolled around on the pebbles, each step stirring up plumes of coffee-colored silt. I tightened my grip on Jim Boy, pulling him along as we waded under the bridge. I stopped for a minute, showing him the pigeons sleeping on the bridge supports.

I sloshed carefully, trying not to think of what might be lurking in the murky water. Maybe a piece of glass or a stray snake that was not resting. There might even be a snapping turtle. I knew the black folk over in Southtown loved to catch those turtles. Annie Barton, our grandmother's maid, said snapping turtle soup was delicious.

"I'm scared," whimpered Jim boy. I was too, but I saw Emeline waiting on the creek bank just beyond, and I'd die before I'd let her know.

"Come on Jim Boy, I'll help you," said Emeline sweetly, reaching out her hand to pull my little brother from the creek. I grabbed a root and pulled myself up.

"What are we going to play?" I asked.

"Let's play revival," said Emeline.

Warming up to Emeline's suggestion, Jim Boy said, "Yeah, let's play revival."

"That's stupid," said Randy. But he went with the rest of us to a ramshackle tool shed behind their house. There were vines growing on the building, and it looked creepy and snaky, but we followed Emeline and Jim Boy inside.

"Now I'm the preacher," said Emeline in her bossiest voice, "and we're going to sing and I'm going to preach."

She stood on an overturned wooden crate, the kind that bottles of Coca-Cola come in, waving her arm to lead the singing. We didn't know much besides "Jesus Loves Me," and "Jesus Loves the Little Children." Well, I knew them. Jim Boy moved his mouth and the other two didn't go to church very much so they sort of hummed along.

Then Emeline began to preach. "I'm talking about sin," she yelled. "I'm talking about plagues and pestilences that come when you sin. I'm telling you that sin chokes you and kills you dead." Emeline was really getting into her sermon when she stepped too close to the edge of the Coca-Cola crate. It tipped and Emeline fell into her congregation of three sitting cross-legged on the dirt floor.

"Damn it to hell!" she screeched.

I laughed, and Emeline's blue eyes blazed. "Well, it's your turn now, Miss Smarty," she said. "I led the singing and I preached, and now it's your turn to get baptized," she said right in my face.

"Okay," I said, "how do we do that?"

"Well, we all get down in the creek and Randy will put a little water on you so you can get saved."

"How much?" I said, having doubts about this whole thing.

"Just a teeny bit," Emeline assured me. "We'll just splash you a little bit. Me and Randy has seen a hundred baptizings up at Grandma Crouch's church at Boaz."

We all climbed down into the creek, except Jim Boy. Emeline said he could sit on the bank and be a believer. We stepped into a pool that was up to my knees. My heart was thumping faster and faster. Suddenly, Randy put an elbow around my neck while Emeline jerked my feet out from under me. I went under for a second, long enough to get a mouthful of the creek water. I spit the water toward my baptizers.

They both stood above me laughing. I sat on the creek bottom, yelling the worst thing I knew, "Butt holes, you shitty buttholes!"

Instinctively, I looked toward the creek bank for Jim Boy. He was running for home, just about to cross Wilson Road. "Jim Boy, stop!" I yelled. I didn't need him running home till my sundress dried a little in the sunshine.

He heard me and stopped. While Randy and Emeline looked at him, I pushed Randy as hard as I could. He fell back into the water, screeched loudly and came up holding his hand. I could see blood beginning to ooze from a cut.

Emeline sloshed over to inspect the wound. "Here Randy, honey, I'll help you," she crooned as she put an arm around his shoulder and helped him out of the ditch. Randy stared at the wound, wide-eyed and sobbing. Emeline sat him down in the shade of a mulberry tree and ran to the house. Soon she appeared with an old white rag. She tied the rag around Randy's hand, which soon absorbed enough blood to look like the stains on the white apron that Uncle Bill wore at the meat market. "See what you did," she snarled at me.

"Look at me," I said. "My sundress and my hair's all wet. Mama will kill me. That was some trick you and Randy pulled on me."

I could see a smirk on her face, but Randy was not laughing yet. Jim Boy came over and said, "l know what, let's eat some wild strawberries."

Emeline rolled her eyes. "All right, go ahead, but they're poison. I know somebody who ate some and died."

"So what can we do?" Jim Boy asked innocently.

"I know," said Emeline. "Let's throw rocks at Aunt Maudie's chickens."

Aunt Maudie lived on the other side of Randy and Emeline's house, away from the creek. The old lady had a fence in her backyard where she kept a flock of red-colored chickens. I liked her a lot because she gave us those fancy cookies that came stacked in a tin box in red crinkly paper cups.

"We can't do that," I said. "That's too mean."

The idea of meanness took Randy's mind off his cut hand. "Okay," he said. "Let's do it."

The four of us picked up some clinkers from their driveway that was paved with cinders from the coal stove. Emaline spotted a big flat rock and gave it to Jim Boy. "Here, honey," she said, "throw this nice rock as hard as you can."

Always eager to please, Jim Boy hefted the stone in both hands, twisted his frame, and threw it with all his might. The stone flew to the top of the fence, but not high enough to clear it. The fence became a slingshot that flung the stone back with a mighty heave. The stone bounced once on the ground, then smashed right on top of Emeline's bare foot.

"Oh, God, I'm dying," she screamed. She rolled in the driveway, holding her foot and getting louder every second. "I'll be a cripple forever." The gritty cinders were sticking to her back and arms as she rolled back and forth in the driveway.

Jim Boy stood by, pale and shocked. His lips trembled.

Emeline's mother, Paulette, stuck her head out the back door to see what the commotion was all about. When she saw her daughter writhing on the ground, she dropped the tall can of Schlitz in her hand and ran down the wooden steps faster than I'd ever seen her move.

She knelt over Emeline, who was still screaming. "Oh baby, tell me what happened. Are you all right?"

Emeline pointed to her second toe. I could see that it was already swelling. "That monster broke my toe," yelled Emeline, pointing a finger at Jim Boy who was backing away.

"And that brat hurt my hand," yelled Randy, pointing at me and showing Paulette the rag Emeline had wrapped around the wound.

"We're going right over to see your mother," Paulette announced. Come on, every last one of you."

Randy led the way. Emeline limped along, and Jim Boy and I hung back. Paulette shooed us along like a flock of turkeys. She got madder with each step.

We waited for a cement truck to pass, and then took giant steps as we crossed Wilson Road because it was so hot and blistery on our bare feet, all except Emeline who was still limping. Paulette ignored our mama's red verbena, marched up the front steps, and called, "Sadie, Sadie, get yourself out here right now."

Our mama came to the door, cautiously.

"Sadie, look here what your kids have done to mine today. Randy is cut to pieces and Emeline's toe is broke. Seems like every time your kids come around something bad happens," she raged.

Our little mama became a banty rooster on the porch. Fire came into her eyes and she puffed up her body to look bigger and meaner. "And what did your kids do to mine?" she yelled. "Janis is as wet as a drowned rabbit and Jim Boy is pale as a ghost."

"Come here, honey," she said to me. I pushed past Paulette and clung to my mama's arm. Jim Boy rushed over, too.

"I'll thank you to tell your kids to leave mine alone," said Paulette as she backed off the porch.

"Gladly!" snapped Mama, seeming somewhat relieved that Paulette was leaving.

We went inside the house. Mama nearly had a fit when she heard that I'd been pushed down in the creek and got nasty creek water in my mouth. "Oh my," she said, "you'll have to have a tetanus shot."

Mama looked at our cousin, whose hair was rolled up with bobby pins by now. "Nona, I need you to watch Jim Boy while I take Janis down to Dr. Neeley's office." Nona nodded "yes," but her eyes were red, and she looked like she'd been crying.

"Oh this is one of the worst days," said Mama. "The preacher came by wanting me to lead the Bible school at church this summer and I was late getting the neutralizer on Nona's permanent. I'm afraid it's going to be too tight, and Nona's all upset. And now this!"

I was feeling kind of sick to my stomach thinking what was going to happen to me when Mama remembered to ask how we got to Emeline and Randy's yard.

Mama let out a long breath, like a sigh. "Nothing good has happened all day long," she said with a sad shake of her head.

"Oh, yes it has," said Jim Boy brightly. "Just be glad that me and Janis got home before the snakes came out."

Pretty Bubbles

My little brother Jim Boy thought Doris Day was a goddess. He especially loved her hit song, "I'm Forever Blowing Bubbles." He listened to it on the jukebox at Uncle Bud's roadhouse on the Montgomery Highway a few miles below Birmingham, Alabama. With his blonde hair and big blue eyes, sweet little Jim Boy was really good at getting customers to drop a nickel in the jukebox so he could hear the Hollywood goddess sing his favorite song.

Uncle Bud's wife, Aunt Dee, was our favorite; she gave us much more freedom than our parents or grandparents ever did. Uncle Bud and Aunt Dee's country farmhouse, just across the highway from the roadhouse, was the best place ever for our summer visit. Our favorite aunt was a free spirit who wore boots most of the time, but never a bra. Her over-permed dye-dark hair was seldom tidy, but her brown eyes twinkled with joy at the antics of dogs and kids.

Aunt Dee had lots of dogs, but her special favorite dog was Smoky, a black cocker spaniel. It was a happy day for us when Smoky produced a litter of six beautiful puppies. We each claimed a puppy as our own, although our parents wouldn't let us bring them back to our home in the city. Jim Boy picked a little black and white pup. "Her name is Bubbles," he proclaimed.

"What a goofy name," I said. As the older sister, I had cleverly named a solid black puppy, my pick of the litter, the descriptive name of Inky.

For once, Jim Boy stood up to his bossy older sister. "I named her Bubbles because she has black circles like bubbles on her white fur. So there!"

We were sitting cross-legged in Aunt Dee's backyard playing with the puppies. Smoky, glad to have a rest, abandoned her little family to the doting brother and sister. Jim Boy picked up the spotted puppy, holding her up so they were face-to-face. In a tuneless croak, he sang to her, "I'm forever blowing bubbles, pretty bubbles in the air. They fly-eye so high..."

"Stop, stop," I screamed. "You can't sing!"

With a hurt look, he stopped singing and finished the serenade in a whisper, mouthing the words in little Bubbles' floppy speckled ears. Smiling smugly, I stroked the already wavy curls on Inky's black fur and wished that the summer of puppies would never end.

Of course, summer ended, and so did our dreams of taking the two puppies home. Our parents' refusal brought many tears. "Why, why, why can't we have the puppies?" I wailed to Aunt Dee.

Aunt Dee was a busy farmer with more than puppies to worry about. She'd been to the barn to feed a little calf whose mother's milk had dried up. On her way back, she came over to sit beside me and Jim Boy and the puppies. "I want to thank you for taking such good care of these puppies this summer. Smoky sure appreciates it, too. But one of them is going to a new home tomorrow. My friend, Adora, is coming to pick up the black and white pup."

"You mean Bubbles?" cried Jim Boy. "No, no, she can't have her!"

Aunt Dee couldn't stand to hear us cry, so she left, forgetting to pick up the empty glass jug that once contained milk for the hungry calf. Little Bubbles, first to spot the white glaze of milk remaining in the gallon jug, waddled over, stuck her head inside and began licking drops of milk, her little pink tongue working like a thirsty sponge.

"She's so cute," said Jim Boy.

I had to agree. But when Bubbles finished her snack of milk and tried to remove her head, the mouth of the jug circled her little neck as firmly as an unwelcome puppy collar. Bubbles struggled and whimpered. Jim Boy, talking soothingly to Bubbles, tried to get her free. Next, I tried, as Bubble's frantic breathing steamed up the inside of the jug.

Ever bossy, even in an emergency, I told Jim Boy, "Quick, quick, go in the house and get Aunt Dee."

Soon, the two came running back, Aunt Dee carrying a hammer. With one sharp whack, she shattered the jar. With another, she broke the mouth of the jar that was stuck on Bubble's neck. Aunt Dee had saved the precious pup.

The next day was a bad day when Adora in her big Hudson sedan arrived from Birmingham to pick up Bubbles. Aunt Dee and Adora walked over as we jealously guarded the pile of pups.

"Oh, aren't they just darling!" Adora exclaimed in her cigarette basso voice. I wondered why someone would wear a green crepe dress with a plunging neckline to pick up a puppy. Didn't the woman own any blue jeans?

As she bent over to pick up Bubbles, Jim Boy's big blue eyes bugged out of his head as the motion exposed too much of Adora's breasts to a little kid who already noticed such things. She squeezed the puppy tightly in her arms. At that, Bubbles peed a warm, wet circle on that too fancy dress. Adora squealed, dropping the puppy sprawling to the ground. How I wished Aunt Dee had said, "You can't have that puppy if you treat her like that." But, Of course, she didn't.

Jim Boy and I sniveled as the Hudson carried his dear Bubbles to an uncertain life in Birmingham with a new owner who we suddenly disliked intensely.

Many years have passed since the summer of puppies. That little brother and I are now senior citizens and nothing is left of that golden time except our memories. But why does grown up Jim have to remember every conversation?

Not long ago, as we recalled those days of happy puppies rolling in the grass and sweet puppy kisses, he said to me, "You really did hurt my feelings when you said I couldn't sing."

Invisible Woman

When Chrissie reserved the round table at Ricardo's Grill for her gang's monthly birthday luncheon, Chef Ricardo smiled broadly and rubbed his hands together in delight as he began his favorite mantra, "Cha-ching, cha-ching." Chrissie and her free spending, wine guzzling pals were money in the bank for Ricardo's constant cash flow problem.

I watched as the boyishly handsome Ricardo rushed to the door to welcome Chrissie's party of four with hugs and elaborate courtesy. "Welcome to Ricardo's Grill," he gushed. "Please follow me on the red carpet to your special table. It's already set with two bottles of my best merlot, on the house from me to my favorite ladies!"

"Oh, Ricardo, you are too kind," cooed Chrissie, preening and looking around to see if other patrons might have noticed their dazzling arrival.

The four friends swept past the other diners. Each of the four wore the uniform dress of the fifty-something, country-club crowd in our town: designer jeans, bright sparkly tops, and manicured toes peeping out of strappy spike-heeled shoes. The subtle coloring on their trendy hair styles was a testament to money well spent; there was not a gray hair in sight.

The owner of the local funeral parlor and a couple of lawyers sitting nearby had indeed noticed their arrival, but not with the appreciation Chrissie desired. "For God's sake, let's get out of here before those girls get any more obnoxious," sniped the eldest of the legal beagles. With a nod to the ladies, the men got up and headed for the door.

I had stopped by Ricardo's for his famous tomato aspic salad after a lengthy meeting with my accountant. Although I was sitting alone at a nearby table, Chrissie looked through me as if I were a gray ghost. To her, I was just a silver-haired old lady wearing comfortable shoes, silver cane hooked on a vacant chair. If she only knew that many of us old folks have learned to see, hear, and keep our mouths shut.

Being invisible to Chrissie and her guests made listening to their table talk a lot easier. I expected their conversation to be like a soap opera fueled by merlot, but what I overheard was more like an expensive Broadway play doomed to end badly.

"Ricardo, darling, come pour our wine," called Sylvia, waving an empty stemmed glass. "After all, it's my thirty-ninth birthday today!" The other three chuckled at Sylvia's little joke.

Chrissie sneered, "Sylvia, darling, the last time you saw thirty-nine was twenty years ago."

As he poured the wine, rolling the bottle to avoid drips after filling each glass, Ricardo asked if they were ready to order. "Heavens no," Sylvia protested. "Our wine can wait no longer."

Chrissie snarled again. "Don't forget that I'm the hostess today I'll decide when we order."

Sylvia glared at Chrissie, raising the glass to her lips for a long, soothing swallow.

After the ladies knocked back their first glasses of wine, Chrissie poured the next round. Marilyn, the quiet one of the group, spoke up. "Listen, girls, I need to order some food. I'm feeling this wine already."

"Marilyn, honey, what's happened to you?" Chrissie mumbled. "Can't you hold your wine?"

"Sorry, Chrissie, I thought we were here to have a nice lunch with food and such."

Just to be sure the others knew she was in charge, Chrissie said, "Okay, I'll call Ricardo."

Ricardo rushed to the table. With any other group he would have told them, "I'll call your waiter," but this group would help him pay his cook and the waiter this week.

I was surprised when the waiter delivered today's menu to my table near the four friends. For the first time ever, Ricardo had given the entrees very fancy French-sounding names. I couldn't help but chuckle at Ricardo's savvy. He seemed to know that his status-conscious patrons would love a menu *en Francais*. It surely was no accident that the elevated prices on today's wine list were intended to cover the cost of the two 'free' bottles of merlot. Ricardo was barely making ends meet, but he was no dummy. He could hardly contain his joy when the ladies' order included two more bottles of wine. And then two more.

When the food arrived, the small talk ended. Chrissie, waving a fork full of food at her other pal, said, "Bunny, pour us another glass of that wine." Bunny smiled, splashing maroon liquid into the glasses and dropping a big red blob on Ricardo's white tablecloth.

"No more for me," said Marilyn, hand over her empty glass. "Two's my limit."

"Marilyn, have you turned into a wimp?" Chrissie smirked.

After three glasses of wine, Chrissie was loosening up enough to get personal. "My mother is driving me crazy," she confided to the girls in a voice so loud I could hear her over at my table.

"Why, what's she doing?" asked Sylvia, with a slight slurring of her words.

"She goes around saying exactly what she thinks. It's so embarrassing."

"I like your mother," said Marilyn. "I think she's just delightful."

'You would, you goody-goody," whispered Chrissie toward Sylvia, getting more irritated by the minute.

"Well, that's just the half of it. She's dating a man not much older than I am, and she's fucking seventy-five."

"Is he rich?" asked Bunny, eyes barely able to focus.

"Is he handsome?" asked Sylvia, eager for details.

"Dammit, he's both!" shouted Chrissie, no longer able to filter her language.

Then Sylvia asked the bombshell question, "Do you think they're doing it?"

"Hell, yes. They're going on a cruise together next month. Can you imagine a seventy-five- year- old grandmother screwing around with a younger man?"

"So what's wrong with your mother having a life?" asked Marilyn. "I think it's really nice she has a good companion."

"I'll tell you what's wrong," screeched Chrissie. "I can't get her to help me with the kids at all. Any time I ask, she's always busy. And furthermore, she's spending my inheritance. Larry and I wanted to buy a cabin on the lake with my share of her money. But she's spending every dime before I get a penny."

"You think you've got problems with your mother?" asked Bunny. My mother is eighty-five, and she just bought a brand-new Tesla, a red one. I think she's losing her mind. She's driving me to drink. Hand me that bottle, Sylvia."

Sylvia, nearly dropping the almost empty bottle, added her bit. "My parents got divorced after forty years of marriage. It's true they hated each other, but why not stick it out for the few years they have left?"

Marilyn chimed in, "So, are they still alive? How are they doing?"

"Mom has never been happier in her life, and Dad has this crazy girlfriend. I'm absolutely humiliated at the way old people behave."

"Don't you mean *misbehave*?" snarled Chrissie.

At last the waiter cleared the table. Bunny's empty wine glass lay on its side. Sylvia, elbows on the table, propped her head up with both hands. Chrissie sat mumbling something else about her mother, her words now muted by alcohol consumption.

I was shocked at the spectacle of three wasted women, drowsy with drink. Chrissie was digging in her Chanel handbag, obviously searching for her credit card to pay the check. Marilyn, looking worried, was surely wondering how she could get this lot home without police involvement.

For once, I was glad to be the invisible old lady sitting at the nearby table. I'd heard too much. I was sad for these young women and even sadder for their mothers.

But my sadness was nothing compared to Ricardo's anguish. The credit card used by Chrissie to pay for the lavish meal and fine wine was declined. Ricardo, near tears, wrung his hands. The cook, disappointed by Ricardo's false promises of a paycheck, flung his apron on the floor and stormed out. The young waiter, with college tuition to pay, yelled, "I quit!" and followed the cook out the door.

Then I watched as the sober one made an important decision. Marilyn surveyed the round table where her three friends were slumped in various stages of inebriation. Striding over to Ricardo, she handed him her golden Visa. "Here, use my card. I'll pay for today."

"Bless you for this," said Ricardo, rushing to the credit card machine.

"Wait, I need one more thing from you," ordered Marilyn.

Ricardo turned to face a newly determined Marilyn. "In exchange for my payment, your job is to call a cab to take those three bitches home. I'm leaving!"

Sarah's Dream

Sarah Jane Baird always got up early to make a hearty breakfast for her family. She'd done this chore every day for thirty years, but today she was distracted. She couldn't get that dream off her mind. Rubbing a hand on her forehead, she thought: *Why did I dream of a schoolhouse over at the front pasture? I saw it sitting there clear as day.*

Still yawning, she grabbed kindling from the wood box and bent to toss it in the wood stove. She got the fire built up hot enough to bake her famous cathead biscuits. She'd fry up thick strips of bacon and a dozen sausage patties in a big old iron skillet on top of the stove. Just before the family got to the table, she'd fry a dozen eggs and pour their coffee into big thick white cups.

"Sarey, quit your daydreaming. We're sitting here a'waiting for our breakfast," yelled her husband Walker from their round wooden table in the dining room. Four hungry folks sat in chairs surrounding the table that was already set with eating utensils and a round mold of fresh churned butter. A cut glass bowl of homemade blackberry jelly was just waiting to be spooned onto Sarah's biscuits.

"I'll help you, Mama," said her youngest child, Sadie, grabbing the plate of biscuits off the sideboard in the hot kitchen. Sarah followed with a platter of bacon, sausage and eggs. She and Sadie went back in the kitchen, coming back carrying steaming cups of coffee that they set down at each plate.

Sadie ran into the kitchen one more time to get her Grandpa Henry his glass of buttermilk. "Here you go Grandpa. Now, say the blessing and let's eat."

Grandpa smiled at Sadie. "I love you, you little June Bug."

As she took her seat at the table, Sarah knew what she had to do. Right after the blessing, Sarah took over. "I think it's time our Claysville community had a real schoolhouse!"

Sarah timed her short speech just right. She had a captive audience in husband, Walker, eleven-year-old Sadie, thirteen-year-old John and Sarah's daddy, Henry Walls.

Yanking a napkin from around his neck, Walker was first to respond. "Well, Sarey, how you gonna pull that off? Country's in a depression and everybody 'round here is poor as church mice."

"Walker, our children have never been to a real schoolhouse. We've got field stones in every hill and holler that other people use for building material. We've got Gus Alred Sr. who's built rock schoolhouses in Guntersville. Why not Claysville?"

"I just say it's bad timing," grumbled Walker.

About that time, Grandpa Henry spoke up from his end of the table. Gulping down the last of his big glass of buttermilk, the old man grinned. "Walker, don't be such a wet blanket. I'll donate the land. Got plenty of it."

Young Sadie, bouncing in her chair, squealed. "A real schoolhouse! Like the folks in Guntersville?"

John spoke up. "Maybe I'd like school a little better if we didn't have to go to school in churches. I'd like to help build it."

Sarah Baird smiled. She knew that her little Sadie's excitement would spread to other youngsters in the community who'd never gone to a real school. "All us kids will pick up the rocks," said Sadie.

"We'll build a mountain of rocks!" bragged John.

Depression or not, Sarah knew that the folks in Claysville would come up with free labor, a few dollars here and there, and maybe even spare building supplies to get that schoolhouse built. Best of all, Sarah knew that Molly Alred would have no trouble convincing her builder husband, Gus Sr., to build the new school. Their two sons, Gus Jr. and George would be among the first students.

Gus Sr. drew up plans for the original four classrooms and auditorium. He and his regular crew plus volunteers worked hard all during 1929 to have the building ready for the first day of school in September of 1930.

Not much book learning happened on opening day of Claysville School. The kids loved their palace of stone, stones they had gathered; enough stones to cover the building with a big pile left over.

Sarah could see the new school from the front porch of the family farmhouse. Sitting nearby, Grandpa Henry said, "I swear Sarah, it looks like a mirage."

To Sarah, the Claysville School looked like a dream come true.

The Claysville School has been the pride of the Claysville community for ninety-four years. The original building, expanded over the years to accommodate a growing population, lies on the main channel of Guntersville Lake. That parcel of donated land has become a valuable piece of real estate. The initial investment in Claysville School was $14,000 dollars. Just recently, the building and some twenty acres was listed for almost ten million dollars. I wonder if Sarah Baird is watching all this from her perch in heaven.

Baby Snooks, I Love You!

My younger brother Jim Boy and I grew up listening to radio shows. Our family didn't even have a TV until 1953, but we didn't care. We loved our radio shows.

We would sit cross-legged on the rug in front of the big, wooden Philco radio set, eyes wide as we waited for Sky King and his niece Penny to spot a gang of rustlers as Sky masterfully piloted his low-flying Cessna over his Arizona ranch.

Sometimes, I almost wet my pants rather than leave at the exciting part when Sergeant Preston of the Yukon was close to saving the lives of two gold miners stranded in a fierce Arctic blizzard. I could just see his dogsled, led by the sergeant's faithful malemute, Yukon King, swishing over deep snow. At the sergeant's sharp command, "On you huskies!" Jim Boy and I knew that lives would be saved and the hearty member of the Royal Canadian Mounted Police would win again.

Of all the radio shows we listened to and enjoyed, none was more beloved than "Baby Snooks." The two of us could hardly wait for Sunday night at 6:30 p.m. when the "Baby Snooks" show came on the air. Jim Boy and I howled with laughter when Baby Snooks tricked her parents every week. One time her report card mysteriously disappeared. Another time she hid a beehive in the living room where her mother was hosting a club meeting.

Jim Boy and I never liked going to the doctor because it usually meant we got a shot, usually in the butt. Just like us, Baby Snooks didn't like going to the doctor. We couldn't stop laughing the time she and her daddy sat waiting in the doctor's office. The x-ray machine caught the attention of Baby Snooks.

"Will it take my picture?' she asked.

"Not that kind of picture," Daddy said.

The always curious Baby Snooks began punching buttons on the X-ray machine until it blew up with a loud bang. Daddy exclaimed, "Now, you've done it! Promise me that you will apologize to the doctor and explain what happened."

"Oh yes, Daddy, I will."

At that point, the doctor rushed into the examination room. Seeing the damage, he was irate. "What have you done to my $5,000 dollar X-ray machine?"

Daddy looked to Baby Snooks. Although we couldn't see her, we were sure that our favorite little girl batted her eyes and began her story. "Well, you see, doctor, we waited so long for you that Daddy got mad and kicked your X-ray machine. He's really sorry."

"Get out, get out," screamed the doctor. And Baby Snooks didn't have to get a shot that day.

Jim Boy and I thought this was hilarious. Why didn't my sweet little brother and I have the nerve to try the tricks that Baby Snooks got by with every Sunday evening?

Sometimes Jim Boy and I sat in our backyard treehouse and talked. Sometimes we talked about parents or friends; sometimes it was the radio shows. One day my little brother asked me, "Why do you like Baby Snooks so much?"

Eighteen months older and much wiser than Jim Boy, I said, "I like her because she is always outsmarting the grownups."

"By being cute," added Jim Boy.

"Why do you like her so much?"

"I like her because she's a little girl about my age," said Jim Boy.

Then came the terrible news one Sunday evening when we took our place in front of the radio. The announcer came on and said, "We regret to inform you that Fannie Brice died today. There will be no more Baby Snooks."

We began sobbing so loudly that our mother rushed in to see what caused our tears. "Baby Snooks is dead," I wailed. "The announcer said it on the radio."

Big tears pouring down his pudgy cheeks, Jim Boy sobbed. "The man said, 'No more Baby Snooks.' Does that mean forever?'"

Then Mother knelt beside us on the rug, a comforting arm around each of us. She gently explained that Baby Snooks was not a real person. She was performed by an actress, a grown-up lady who pretended to be a little girl. It's Fannie Brice who died, not baby Snooks.

"No, no, she's real," he insisted.

"I thought you knew it was just a comedy show on the radio," Mother said. "I'm so sorry for the bad news."

Later that night, Jim Boy and I lay awake in our twin beds in our cozy blue bedroom. I was trying to work out in my mind how Baby Snooks could be an actress and a little girl at the same time. I heard my little brother sobbing quietly in his bed.

"What is it, Jim Boy?"

"I'm crying because Mother said that Baby Snooks is not a real little girl. She's wrong! Baby Snooks is real. And now she's dead." This brought on more sobs. I got up and gave him a tissue. He wiped his eyes and loudly blew his nose.

Sniffling, Jim Boy threw off his blanket and crawled to the foot of his bed where there was a window. Looking out into the night sky with twinkling stars and a sliver of moon, he whispered his farewell.

"Good-bye Baby Snooks. I'll love you forever."

Blue Bronco

Back in 1965 when headlines about the war in Vietnam dominated the news, a smaller, more personal conflict raged between eighteen-year-old Edwin and his steady girlfriend Jess, who was the same age but had a different mindset. For Edwin, the idea of leaving Jess and home was scary, but the Vietnam War was raging. Edwin thought joining the Army after graduation might be better than waiting to be drafted. Jess was fixed on the notion that she and Edwin would get married that summer and live happily ever after in their hometown of Sneedville in the mountains of upper East Tennessee.

Jess was tired of hearing Edwin fret about getting drafted. "Get that silly notion out of your head. There's no way our draft board would take you away from here. Let's go ahead and get married just like we planned," she insisted.

Just who was planning to get married this summer? Maybe in a couple of years, but not now. With all the pressure from Jess plus the fear of the draft, Edwin was beginning to feel like a June bug with a string tied to his leg. "Honey, watch the six o'clock news tonight. The body count gets higher every day. Our soldiers are getting blown up in tanks and ambushed in the jungles. Don't you realize I could get sent over there and come back in a box?"

Jess just rolled her eyes, dismissing her sweetie as if he were a child, but tall, athletic Edwin was not a child. He was star forward on the basketball team, a hometown hero who also ran track and cross country. In summers he coached younger boys playing church league baseball. Life was good for Edwin. There was comfort in playing sports. He liked being looked up to by his young players. He liked being a hometown hero. Given a choice, he would never leave Sneedville and the life and people he loved.

Jess, a straight A student, presided over Beta Club and excelled in every cooking and sewing project of the Future Homemakers of America. She and her friends in Future Homemakers and her Sunday school class spent hours talking about wedding plans, much as their mothers before them had done. Jess was an only child accustomed to getting her way. No way would she let Edwin slip away. They were an ideal couple. Everybody said so.

The tension between Edwin and Jess was complicated by plain old teenage hormones. Edwin strutted around school wearing tight jeans that showed off his trim butt and an even tighter white tee-shirt showing bulging arm and chest muscles. He confided to Jess that he was always horny.

Jess did a good job of convincing her classmates and her doting parents that she was a wholesome, nice, church-going girl, which she was, but her hormones were surging just like her boyfriend's. Unfortunately, Edwin's plans for their future were several years behind Jess's goal of getting married as soon as possible. She was thinking how nice it would be to make love in their own bedroom. Edwin was perfectly happy to screw around on the scarcely padded bench seat in his blue Bronco.

Edwin was usually agreeable to almost anything Jess wanted. He'd worn his hair in a crew cut most of his life. That all changed one evening when he and Jess cuddled on the sofa in her parents' family room watching the Beatles perform on "The Ed Sullivan Show."

"Edwin, honey, their shaggy hair is so cute. I just love it."

That's all it took for lovesick Edwin to grow out his crewcut to achieve the mop-top look of the boys from Liverpool. Their high school yearbook included a full-page photo of Edwin, complete with floppy bangs, posing for the honor of being elected a senior superlative in two categories: Best Looking Boy and Most Athletic.

Jess's full-page in the yearbook lauded her as Most Popular Girl. Her picture featured a confident-looking young woman with a pleasant face, free of teenage blemishes. Fellow students who voted her most popular knew that the girl in the picture exactly matched the friendly girl they saw by the locker every morning. Always neatly dressed, she wore just the right amount of makeup, a simple necklace and, of course, Edwin's senior ring.

The closer he got to the June graduation date, the more nervous Edwin got about the implied commitment of trading his senior ring for a wedding ring. He loved Jess, but what's the hurry to get married? He knew the Army was in his future, either by draft or enlisting, and this meant leaving behind his home and his girlfriend for a couple of years. Jess was talking wedding bells, selecting silver and china patterns, and deciding on her bridesmaids. The more Jess talked about getting married right after graduation, the more Edwin felt trapped.

How could a guy just out of high school support a wife? With the fighting going on in Vietnam, he knew his draft number was coming up soon. College wasn't on his radar because he didn't know what he wanted to study. He could consider going to college after his Army discharge using his veteran's benefits.

He tried a different tactic with Jess, "Sweetheart, you're really a smart girl. Don't you want to go to college before you get tied down with a husband and kids? You've done so well in school. What's something you'd like to do while I'm in the Army?"

Jess maintained, "I can go to college anytime. I love you, and I just want us to get married."

Edwin tried to reason with her. "One of us has got to be practical. I love you, too, baby, but we can't live on love."

"Oh, Edwin," she pouted, "you are such an old fuddy-duddy! Lots of our friends are getting married, some this summer and a few more around Christmas."

"You're right," he agreed, "but most of those guys have jobs. I've never worked because I've played and coached sports all these years. You deserve more than I could give you right now."

In his mind, Edwin kept flipping a coin. Heads I get drafted; tails I get married. To Edwin, either choice was a death sentence; he could get blown to bits in the war, or he could face a life sentence with a wife and kids before he was ready.

During Spring Career Day in the high school gym, Edwin could hardly wait to talk to the Army recruiter. He stood in a line of about twenty guys eager to discuss their options with the handsome soldier in a starched khaki uniform. While Edwin waited his turn, he looked around the gym and thought, *I love this place. I'm sure gonna miss it.*

He looked around, too, hoping to see Jess talking with recruiters from the college over in Johnson City or maybe the two-year college in Kingsport. He knew she could get a scholarship if she'd only apply.

Finally, Edwin made it to the front of the line, hoping to ask the recruiter his question where the other guys in line couldn't hear.

"What can I tell you about the Army, young man?"

Edwin replied, "Uh, do you think joining up might be better than getting drafted? Uh, what I mean is, would joining up maybe keep me from getting shipped overseas before I could get some job training?"

"I get asked that question a lot. It might help. But it might not. What sort of training did you have in mind?" quizzed the recruiter.

Edwin tried to think of a program that would take the longest, "I'm thinking about something electrical, like wiring and cabling."

"That's a great field, one we really need. Why don't you come down to Knoxville and talk to me once you graduate? I'll help you all I can." Edwin liked that answer. It wasn't a sure thing, but he felt good to have that first step behind him.

Just a couple of weeks later, back in the gym on a hot evening in early June, he and Jess and fifty of their high school classmates graduated from Newman County High School. Beaming in their caps and gowns, the graduates marched over to the cafeteria for a reception. The Senior Class of 1965 had no interest in eating cake or tasting punch; they were too busy hugging each other, saying their good-byes. Edwin's mother started the picture taking, pulling a Brownie Hawkeye camera from her purse, and reeling in Edwin and Jess for a picture. Next, she captured Edwin with his dad. Finally, Jess's parents grabbed the pair for pictures. And Edwin obliged by taking a picture of Jess with her parents.

"Hey, you two want to come over to the house and have some ice cream and cake?" asked Jess's mom. "Edwin, see if your parents would like to join us."

Jess spoke up, "Oh, I'm so sorry, Mama, but Edwin and I are going to a party."

"Have fun, kids!" she said, covering her disappointment with a brave smile.

Soon the two new graduates were laughing as they headed to their own private party down a dark logging road way up on Newman's Ridge. Before long they were making out big time, fogging up the windows with their heavy breathing. Jess was really turned on and Edwin was certainly not holding back. During a pause in the action, Jess whispered, "Honey, if we get married, we could do this all the time."

"Sweetheart, there's lots of reasons why getting married right now is not a good idea. You know I really need to join the Army so I don't get drafted and sent to Vietnam," he insisted.

"Oh, honey," she sighed. "We could get married now and I'd wait for you."

"Lord, help me, you're awful persuasive when you're sitting on my lap and making hickeys on my neck."

"So let's run off and get married," she whispered.

"Sweetie, what's the matter? You're not knocked up are you," Edwin questioned.

"Of course not, you idiot! You know I'm on the pill." With that, Jess sat up, snapped the hooks closed on her bra and the fight was on.

"Take me straight home," she screeched.

"Sweetie, I didn't mean that to sound like I don't care. We'll get married and have some kids, just not now," he argued.

"Take me home!" Jess exclaimed.

While Edwin revved the engine, Jess reached in her purse for lipstick, making a smacking sound as she smeared frosted pink over her lips. Next, a brush to get that bell-shaped hairdo back in place. She called it a flip. She didn't know what she would do if her mother asked about the beard burns on her cheeks.

Bumping down the logging road, dodging mud puddles, rocks pinging on the Bronco's underside, they finally got back to town. Jess was still not speaking, arms hugging her chest, riding in silence until they reached her house. The door on the Bronco squeaked as she wrenched it open, and she jumped out onto the sidewalk. The door slammed with a sound like a shotgun blast.

During that long night after the breakup, Edwin reached a decision. Next morning, he washed Newman's Ridge mud off his Bronco, pumped it full of gas at the Amoco station on U.S. 11W and drove sixty-nine miles to Knoxville where he enlisted in the U.S. Army.

"War is hell," he decided, "but getting married is worse!"

Frozen Pane

My younger brother Jim Boy and I hardly noticed the chill in the air as our parents loaded up the family car in Birmingham for a 250-mile drive farther north to our new home in Oak Ridge, Tennessee. We were too excited. Our daddy, a skilled machinist, had a new job in the government's weapons plant in a town known as 'the Atomic City' in the hills of East Tennessee.

The movers emptied our house the day before and headed north to set up our new home before we arrived. "Won't that be nice to have our own beds to sleep in tonight?" asked mother, knowing that we had a long drive ahead of us on winding two-lane roads, well before the advent of interstate highways.

With every mile we traveled, the temperature dropped, first to freezing weather and finally to an Arctic blast.

Jim Boy and I were thrilled as the windows on the 1950 Chevrolet clouded over from the cold outside and the foggy breath of four people inside. In seven-year-old scrawl, Jim Boy wrote his name in the moisture on his side of the car. As the older sister, I wrote my name on my window in newly learned cursive. I was nine years old.

Then we both started drawing on the misty windows, trying to be quiet so our parents wouldn't make us stop.

"What are you children doing?" asked our mother, turning around from her vantage point in the front seat.

"Nothing," answered Jim Boy, "just looking out the window at icicles on those pretty rocks we're passing."

"I'm getting cold," said mother with a little shiver. "Are you kids warm enough?"

"It's a little chilly," I said. "But we're okay."

Daddy, looking worried, busily dodged icy spots on the highway as we passed through one little town after another in Alabama. Finally, he said, "I'd turn up the heat, but the damn heater has stopped working."

When Daddy drove up the steep ridge in Chattanooga, we knew we were in our new state, closer to Oak Ridge with every passing mile. It was so cold by now that the moisture on the backseat windows froze in white sheets. Two bored young travelers started making handprints on the icy windows and scratching pictures with our fingernails. Oh, it was great fun — until it wasn't. That's when Jim Boy got the bright idea to lick the window with his moist pink tongue. Guess what? His tongue stuck to the frozen window like a wad of used bubble gum sticks to a shoe.

My brother made strange noises and frantically waved his arms. His tongue was not coming loose. First, I thought it was funny, then I got scared.

"Mother, can you help? Jim Boy's tongue is stuck to the window."

"What in heaven's name?" she swore in a panic.

By that time, my brother was crying, and I didn't much blame him.

The warm tears must have helped. At last, his tongue broke loose. The icy glass had marked my little brother's tender tongue with an angry-looking freezer burn.

Reaching over the seat to comfort her still frightened son, Mother examined the injury. "Oh, honey, are you feeling better now?" Jim Boy nodded his head, tears still glistening in his big blue eyes.

But Jim Boy's dilemma was minor compared to what happened next. It was late afternoon. The whole family was cold and tired. Suddenly, I heard Daddy swear a string of unprintable words.

Daddy had spotted our moving van stalled in the road; the problem was obvious. A swirling river of muddy water roared over the final bridge on the road to Oak Ridge. We were in sight of Oak Ridge, but getting up the steep hill to our new home would be impossible until the water receded.

The moving van and its crew, as well as my family, were all stuck in Oliver Springs, a small country town in the flat land below the ridge. Daddy got out of the car and stood in the roadway. He raised his hands in frustration. "Welcome to GOL DARN paradise!" he yelled.

Only he didn't say "GOL DARN!"

Love the One You're With

Heavy-fisted banging on the warped screen door at Mama Liza and Grandpop's house scared me out of a sound sleep. Bang, bang, bang! The noise got louder as the old wooden door slammed against the door frame. Someone out there in the night wanted inside really badly. I pulled the pile of quilts over my head.

Grandpop, hearing the banging, stormed down the hall. The lid on the candy dish rattled as he rushed through the living room on his way to the front door. Feeling much safer, I threw back the quilts and tip-toed over to my bedroom door, opening it just wide enough for safe spying. About that time Grandpop arrived at the front door, grasping his long-barreled revolver in both hands. I saw him peer through the glass on the front door, sizing up the intruders.

As Grandpop slid back the bolt lock with a click and eased open the door, his son, my daddy, bellowed, "Let us in! We need something to eat." I watched my daddy stagger inside his parents' house. Usually, when I looked at my tall, handsome daddy, I was proud; tonight, he looked more like a blurry picture of himself. I was ashamed. Even from my bedroom door, I got a big whiff of cigarettes and whiskey.

"Son, it's the middle of the night," said Grandpop, lowering the revolver. He didn't look much like a security guard in his white one-piece underwear. With no pocket to stash the firearm, he eased it behind his back. But from the looks of my daddy, I don't think he noticed the gun.

"Who's that with you?" asked Grandpop, squinting to recognize the figures on the dark porch.

That's when Daddy's friend Billie Jean wobbled inside. "How you doing, Mr. Astin?" she slurred. "We was hoping your sweet wife would fix us some breakfast."

Billie Jean reached out the door to drag her tall, slim husband Ralph inside as if he were a piece of flexible hose. Ralph, Daddy's best friend, had just come home to Birmingham after two years overseas fighting the Germans.

While my daddy and his pals stood swaying, Mama Liza appeared. Wearing a floral bathrobe and a pink hairnet, she was a frightening figure. She glared at Daddy with her look that meant big trouble. He lurched backward, almost as if he'd been swatted with her broom. "Guess we better be going," he mumbled.

"I guess you had," she said in a voice chillier than the night air.

"Be careful, Son," said Grandpop, as he flipped on the porch light.

I could hear the tires on Daddy's Ford coupe throwing gravel as he backed the old car out the driveway and roared away on the dark winding Wilson Road. Getting back under my quilts, I lay awake and prayed that my daddy would be okay. "Please, Lord, help him not to drink anymore tonight. And please keep my daddy safe. I'm scared, Lord. Amen."

As my grandparents walked together to their bedroom, Mama Liza peeped into my bedroom while Grandpop looked in on my little brother in the next room. I pretended to be asleep; sweet little Danny, I think, had slept through the whole thing. I could hear Mama Liza whisper a little too loud, "I wonder if Beth knows that woman is with Sonny and Ralph tonight?"

"I just don't understand it," he answered sadly.

"But Beth acts like she's crazy about him. Calls him her sweetheart," said Mama Liza. "Does she not know?"

"Maybe he'll grow up one day," said Grandpop.

At breakfast the next morning, I was telling Danny all about our daddy's nighttime visit. Mama Liza, listening as she stirred our oatmeal, said, with a scowl, "Karen, I don't think he needs to hear all that."

But it was too late. The five-year-old looked up innocently from his chair at the kitchen table. "I wish I could have seen Miss Billie Jean. She's so pretty. Daddy thinks so, too."

Mama Liza rolled her eyes. "Danny, honey, how do you know Miss Billie Jean?"

"Oh, me and Daddy and Karen go see her every week. Didn't you know Mr. Ralph asked Daddy to look out for her and Ralph Jr. while he was away at the war?"

"Is that right?" asked Mama Liza, pouring oatmeal into our two favorite Fiesta Ware bowls, blue for Danny and yellow for me.

"Sure thing," said Danny, "Daddy helps her with things she needs inside the house and me and Karen play outside in the old dairy with Ralph Jr."

"How nice," said our grandmother.

Our parents came to pick up Danny and me right after lunch. I always hated to leave Mama Liza and Grandpop's house. It was so peaceful there in the big kitchen that smelled like cinnamon and warm biscuits. But Danny, squealing with excitement, ran over to Daddy and threw his little arms around him. "Daddy, Daddy, why didn't you wake me up last night? I wanted to see Miss Billie Jean," Danny shouted.

"I'm sorry, buddy, but you were sound asleep," said Daddy with a sheepish look. Mama Liza glared at Daddy.

"Sweetheart, I didn't know you came over here last night," said Mama, looking puzzled.

"It was just for a minute," said Daddy, squirming like a teen-ager getting his first speeding ticket.

By the time I was a teen-ager, I lost interest in Billie Jean and Ralph, but Daddy didn't. He had a good job at the tin mill, where he was now a supervisor in the machine shop. He always seemed to know where his friends were living and what they were doing. He still talked on the phone with Billie Jean fairly often. Did Mama know? If she did, she never said anything.

The years passed quickly. I married a young man I'd met at college. Danny surprised us all by marrying a girl from New York he'd met on a geology field trip. Our parents' twenty-fifth wedding anniversary was observed at a good friend's home; Danny and I were busy with new jobs and our own young children, so we didn't get back to Birmingham for the party.

Decades passed, and Daddy and Billie Jean still exchanged regular phone calls. Once when I was back in Birmingham for a visit, I heard Daddy talking on the phone with Billie Jean. I could hear him asking about the boys, who were both grown and living in Calera, a small Alabama town near Billie Jean and Ralph. Did Mama have feelings about the phone calls that continued over the years? If she did, she kept it to herself.

One day, Daddy called me to say that Ralph had died of a stroke. "He was only fifty-eight."

"I'm really sorry. How is Billie Jean doing?" I asked.

"She sounded real sad when I called her last night. Me and Beth are going to the funeral. I'll let you know how she's doing," he said. "You're welcome to come if you can."

I couldn't help but wonder if Ralph's death would cause Daddy to do something stupid. I hoped not. Was Mama worrying about Daddy's feelings for Billie Jean? Did she even know?

More years passed. Danny and I hosted a big event at a local hotel when Daddy and Mama celebrated their 50th wedding anniversary. The banquet room was filled with friends who'd come to wish them well. One of my friends sang popular songs from the late 1930s when my parents were courting, leading to their wedding in 1939. Although his hair was gray, it was still wavy, and our daddy was as handsome as ever. He hugged and kissed our mama throughout the celebration. Mama, who wasn't quite five-feet tall, told the crowd, "I'm so happy I feel ten-feet tall."

Sometime in the intervening years, a tornado struck the small town where Billie Jean and the boys lived, causing quite a bit of devastation. Mama told me that Daddy was worried sick after he heard the news. "I told him Billie Jean was surely okay or we would have heard something."

Daddy got the big idea to drive over there to check on them, but the emergency management folks were asking people not to come. Mama said Daddy called and called until the phone lines were restored. "After he finally reached her, she told him they only had minor damage."

By the time their 70th anniversary rolled around, both Daddy and Mama were beginning to have health problems. Many of their friends had died, so the celebration was just a small dinner party with a few friends at a local country club. My brother Danny sent red roses, our mama's favorite. My son sent a poem he'd written for the occasion. Daddy stood up and told Mama, "I still love you just as much as I did seventy years ago."

My parents reached their nineties, disabled with health problems to the point they had round-the-clock caregivers. Daddy's heart was failing, limiting his mobility. Mama was growing increasingly forgetful with dementia which robbed her of her dignity. Billie Jean, in her late eighties, suffered from severe arthritis. Still Daddy and Billie Jean talked on the phone at least once a week, sometimes more. The caregivers were curious about this regular caller.

One afternoon, I dropped by their house to check on my parents. Mama appeared to be dozing in her recliner chair. Daddy was in his bedroom taking a nap. Brenda, the daytime caregiver, said, "Karen, I've got a question. Who is that woman who talks on the phone to your daddy so often?"

The question roused my mama sufficiently to answer Brenda's question before I could say a word. "Oh," Mama said brightly, "she's my husband's girlfriend."

Open Mouth, Insert Foot

There is no cure when the plague of senioritis settles on a person and high school graduation is only a few weeks away. My pals, Brenda, Rhonda, and I decided that skipping school and spending the day at a nearby lake might ease the pain.

Brenda and Rhonda just didn't come to school on that beautiful day in May. Skipping school for me required extra effort because my mother worked at the school administration office. She was the sharp-eyed lady who saw the high school absentee list each day, and woe is me if my name appeared on the list without her approval.

So, what is a clever senior to do? I went to school and checked out after the daily absentee list was sent to mother's office. Brenda had forged an excellent note requesting that I be excused for a doctor's appointment. Her mastery of my mother's handwriting was impressive. When the office assistant at the high school called my home to verify that I had an appointment, Brenda answered the phone. "Yes, of course, Sandra has an appointment. She's getting her physical for college."

With the call complete, my friends rushed to pick me up at the gym entrance, where I was less likely to be spotted leaving with someone who was not my parent. Next, we picked up illegal beverages, sandwiches, and maybe even a pack of Pall Malls. And onward we went to a sunny spot on the sparkling lake. What a great day! No one was around to watch as we swam, worked on our tans, and even practiced blowing smoke rings, a skill we were sure to need in college.

We arrived back in town just as if we'd been at school all day. Our parents would never know. Or so I thought. We went to school the next day, smiling smugly. Our little caper had been a big success. The phone rang just as I got home from school. The caller was my mother. "How are you?" she asked.

"Oh, fine, fine," I assured her.

"Well, I just thought I'd let you know that Brenda and Rhonda have been suspended."

"For what?" I screeched.

"For skipping school yesterday," she said.

"But I did it, too! I was with them!"

"That's what I thought," she said with a laugh. "They didn't really get suspended."

I never did know how she found out.

Double Whammy!

Nothing is more demeaning than growing up gay in a small Southern town where the local interpretation of the Bible makes saints of white people and sinners of anyone who is gay, black or a Yankee. I'd tried hard to keep my secret in this backwater town of Yuchi, Mississippi, for fear of being beat up by rednecks or bringing shame to my sweet mama.

Thank goodness, I wasn't a limp-wristed gay boy, so I played the game, dated girls and lettered in the no-contact sports track and baseball at Yuchi High School. Mom knew I was gay, but we never let on to my daddy, who liked nothing better than to tell off-color jokes about queers and niggers.

I'd been wanting to leave for Atlanta right after high school, but Mom shed a few tears and got me to promise that I'd not pack up and leave until finishing four years at Mississippi State, where I had a baseball scholarship. That's an awful long time to keep a secret, but I did it.

Mom was getting nervous when I started my senior year at Starkville. "Son, I don't understand why you are bound and determined to leave us all behind soon as you graduate. Our little town's not all that bad."

"Don't you know, Mom, that folks in Yuchi don't do much more than get born, grow up, go to church twice on Sunday, and drop dead when they're too old to care what their neighbors are doing?" Johnny argued.

"That's awfully harsh, Johnny. You've had a good life here," replied mom.

Years later, I'm a grown man, living the good life in Atlanta with Rob, my long-time love, when Mom calls from Mississippi. "Son, is it okay if I come see you tomorrow? There's something I need to tell you."

"Can't you tell me now, Mom?"

"Do you not want me to come, honey?" Her voice quivered, a sure sign that tears would soon follow.

"You know you're welcome anytime, Mom. Come on over."

"Well, okay, if you're sure. But don't you and Rob go to any trouble now, you hear."

While I racked my brain trying to guess what she wanted, Rob laughed. "Stop spinning your wheels. Just call your brother Charlie. He'll know."

Charlie answered after only a couple of rings. "I thought that might be you," he said. "I guess you want to know Mom's big news item without waiting till tomorrow. Right?"

"You damn right! What's going on?"

"What if I told you that dear old Dad has asked Mom for a divorce? Says he's met a woman he can't live without."

"So, how's Mom taking it?"

"She's mad as hell! This gal is younger than I am. And I think there's some urgency that the wedding take place fairly soon."

"Oh Lord, how can I help?"

"Just listen," advised Charlie, "And when she's done, give her a big hug."

When Rob and I got home from work, she was already parked in our driveway. Her sad face peering through the windshield reminded me of a sweet Lab puppy someone had yelled at.

After hugging us both and shedding a few salty tears on my best silk tie, she followed us into the condo. "Fix me a Sex on the Beach," she ordered. "I've got lots to tell you."

Rob pulled out our best rum and the drink mixers. My hundred-pound Mom dropped limply to the sofa, motioning for me to join her.

"Okay, guys," she said. "My dear husband of thirty-four years wants a quickie divorce so he can marry this cheap little twit who works over at the junior college."

The tears were starting to flow again, so I grabbed a box of Kleenex. "You're kidding me!" I said, acting surprised.

"No, I'm not. That sorry asshole fooled around a couple of times before, but he's always come home with his tail 'a dragging."

Rob handed her the fruity drink. After a few long sips, she took a deep breath and resumed her story.

"It's not that I still love the son of a bitch," she said, punching her fist in the air. "This is just damned embarrassing. Most of the old-timers in town know he got me knocked up my senior year in high school. And now he thinks this little homewrecker might be in a family way."

"Wait! Hold up, Mom. Are you saying I'm a love child? I never knew that."

Covering her face with both hands, she sobbed, "Oh, honey, I'm so sorry. I never meant to tell that."

"Tell me more," I begged.

"How come you think I never showed you our wedding pictures? My wedding dress was a maternity smock 'cause I was five months gone by the time my daddy got that slippery snake to the altar."

"And then I turn out to be gay!"

"That's okay with me," she said. "What I'm pissed about is your sorry shit of a father sneaking around getting this latest girlfriend pregnant. My Daddy threatened to shoot him all those years ago. I wish he had."

"Wow, Mom, that's quite a story. I see why you're mad." I threw my arms around her. "Let me hug your tears away," I whispered.

After a few sniffles, she started laughing. "That's what I used to say to you and Charlie when you were little."

"Rob, sweetheart, fix me another drink," she called, swirling her empty glass.

With only a slight slurring of her words, she said with a wink, "It's high time I told you boys what our dull little town is REALLY like!"

Queen of the Road

Only two people know the secret of why all four tires on my daddy's brand new 1958 Chevrolet Impala sport sedan would not stay inflated. Those people would be me and my car-loving friend, Buddy.

Daddy never knew the truth. All he knew is that each morning when he went out to drive this yellow hardtop beauty to work, all four tires were smashed like busted pumpkins.

The first morning, Daddy stomped the ground and swore, "Those damn kids! Just a bunch of hoodlums. Guess they think deflating tires is funny!" He stormed back inside and got the keys to his 1950 Ford Coupe, tires squealing as he raced off to work.

When he got home from work, Daddy got out his hand pump and worked up a sweat pumping air into those brand-new whitewalls. Watching from the kitchen window, Mama chuckled, "Daddy's having a fit to show off his brand-new Impala to the guys at work."

"I don't blame him, Mama. That's the prettiest car I've ever seen. It's a totally new body design with a Turbo Fire V8 engine."

"Lord, honey, where did you learn all that? I didn't know girls cared all that much about cars."

"Buddy told me. We've been dying to see the new Impala."

Daddy came in for supper. Mama had made Daddy's favorite meal, meatloaf and mashed potatoes, so he was too busy chowing down to talk about the tires.

The next morning, Daddy was whistling as he walked out to his new car. Guess what? All four tires were flat again! "Just wait till I catch those rotten kids!" he screamed.

He stormed back into the house and called Nicky's Tire Service. "Come to my house, inflate these damn tires, and put a cap on the tube nozzles so tight the kids can't get them loose."

Later in the day, Nicky called Daddy at work. "Mr. Jim, those tires won't stay inflated. We need to haul your car to the shop where we can jack that baby up to check each tire."

An hour later, Nicky called again. "Sorry to bother you, Mr. Jim, but every one of your tires is full of mud. They ought to stay inflated once we clean 'em out."

"Wonder how that happened? Wanna bet that car sat on some dealer's muddy lot for a couple of months before I bought it? Go ahead, Nicky, and clean it up. I've only had it for a couple of weeks, and I'm raring to drive it. My daughter is crazy about it, too."

Some sixty years have passed since the mystery of the muddy tires, so now I can tell the real story of how the tires got filled with mud. I was a daddy's girl back then, a junior in high school with a brand new driver's license. "I love that car, Daddy, please, please let me drive it down to the Woodland drugstore where all the cute guys hang out."

"Okay, honey, just be real careful. Don't stay too long."

When I pulled up in that yellow beauty, the guys swarmed over. "Hey, Sandra, open the hood."

"Let's see that engine."

"Wow! How fast will it go?"

I was so proud of that car and all the attention it got me. I wasn't quite ready to go home; so I drove over to Lafayette Drive to take the car for a little spin on the nice straight stretch of highway. I stomped the accelerator. First to forty-five miles per hour, then up to sixty. I'm not sure how fast I was driving the yellow beauty when…whoops! She spun out of control, left the road, skidded down the muddy right-of-way.

I tried everything to get back on the road. The tires were spinning, slinging mud all over the car. I panicked. About that time, my friend Buddy pulled up in his '56 Mercury and jumped out of his car. He laughed like my dilemma was the funniest thing he'd ever seen. "Okay, sport, let's get you out of this mess," he said.

He walked over to a nearby house and asked to use the phone to call a wrecker. Soon, the wrecker arrived, attached a tow chain, jerked once, and I was back on the road. Buddy peeled off some cash and paid the driver. Meanwhile, I stared at a mud-covered car and wondered what would happen next.

Buddy saved my hide. "I'll follow you to the Jiffy Car Wash. We'll clean her up, and your daddy will never know."

But I've always wondered. Whenever we talked about that 1958 Impala, Daddy always grinned. Did that twinkle in his eye tell me he knew all along?

Mississippi Visitation

When Uncle Arthur opened the doors of his funeral parlor on that humid August evening in Yuchi, Mississippi, he knew to step aside quickly to avoid the rush of folks racing to be first inside for the all-night visitation of a beloved young man brought down by a sniper's bullet in the bloody First Battle of Khe Sanh in the Quang Tri Province of Vietnam.

Most of the locals knew that Marine Corporal Ray Anderson's military casket would be closed; they'd never again see the handsome face of the friendly boy who grew up among them, always planning to join the Marine Corps as soon as he graduated from Yuchi High. Ray's dream of service as a Marine died with him thousands of miles from home. Ray's mom, back home in Yuchi, told me that a part of her died that awful day when two solemn Marines came to her door with the tragic news.

I loved Ray's mom Marileigh like a sister. We'd grown up together in Yuchi and couldn't wait to get to Mississippi State College for Women, better known as the W. Oddly enough, going to the W was an expectation, not a choice. Our mothers and all our female relatives were proud graduates of the institution guaranteed to make us gracious ladies.

After college, Marileigh married her high school sweetheart, and returned home to partner with her husband in the family jewelry store. Together they raised two beautiful children, Ray Jr. and Betsy.

I'd had enough of Mississippi by the time I got a B.A. and my Mrs. degree, so my new husband and I migrated across the state line to start a new life in Birmingham, some 135 miles away. The miles didn't matter; Marileigh and I remained dear friends, visiting often and talking on the phone almost every day.

Since my Uncle Arthur owned the funeral parlor, he sneaked me in the backdoor to stand with Marileigh, Ray Sr. and their daughter, Betsy, before the crowd rushed inside. We hugged and cried together. Thank goodness, boxes of tissues were strategically placed throughout the room. I grabbed a handful, handing several to my grieving friends.

When my uncle opened the funeral parlor doors to begin the long night of the visitation, friends and neighbors didn't waste a minute getting inside. Aunt Hazel, carrying her famous Harvey Wallbanger cake, rushed to the hospitality table. "I remember how Ray Jr. loved my cake," she shouted above the noise of shuffling feet and murmured condolences. "This is for him."

The ladies from First Methodist Church brought plates of brownies and gallons of sweet tea. I couldn't tell you how many ladies from the Yuchi Woman's Club brought deviled eggs and finger sandwiches. No one would go hungry during the long night of honoring Ray Jr.

I heard Marileigh whisper to Ray Sr., "Don't you wish Ray Jr. could be standing beside us tonight? He's known these wonderful people all his life."

"No one knows how much I wish he were here," sobbed Ray Sr., so bent with grief, he looked no taller than Betsy, who clung to her father like a snail on a sidewalk.

Teachers, school friends, and neighbors all came to pay their respects. The parlor was soon crowded with hometown folks mingling with Marine Corps friends from everywhere, some brown, some tan, some white, an oddity in these parts.

It wasn't long before our best friend Tinker Allen came through the door with a tight grip on the arm of her elderly daddy. The reverent spell of the visitation was broken temporarily when the old man spotted a sight he'd never seen before in Yuchi, Mississippi. "What's them niggers doing here? Don't they have their own funeral parlor?"

"Hush up, Daddy," said Tinker in a loud whisper. "Be nice, that's some of Ray Jr.'s friends from the Marines."

"Never thought I'd live to see this!" he said, his walking stick swishing the air like an infantry saber. The visiting Marines just smiled, while more than a few of the hometown folks most likely shared Mr. Allen's thoughts, and just didn't say anything.

Mr. Wells, publisher of the *Yuchi Courier*, quietly asked Uncle Arthur for any details he might use in a news story of Ray Jr.'s death. "This will be front page news this week," confided Mr. Wells. "I'm even running a picture of the boy in his dress uniform," he continued.

Uncle Arthur answered with all the skill of a long-time owner of a funeral parlor. "Our Ray died a hero, taking a bullet meant for an eighteen-year-old private."

Mr. Wells, nodding in amazement, scribbled this tidbit in his reporter's notebook.

Uncle Arthur's wife, my Aunt Vinnie, kept a close eye on Ray Jr.'s grieving parents all through the long evening. "There's just so many hugs and kind words those two can endure," she told me. "I'm gonna ask two of those nice Marines to drag a couple of chairs over so Marileigh and Ray Sr., can sit a spell."

By midnight, the funeral parlor was buzzing with the hushed tones of both the mourners and the curious. Miss Viola Barnes and her daughter Crazy Shirley never missed a visitation whether they knew the deceased or not. "There they are," said Aunt Vinnie, "Maybe they don't have a TV."

Crumbs from brownies littered the carpet. Only the bare plate remained of Aunt Hazel's cake. The smell of stale coffee mingled with the nauseating scent of lilies in the floral offerings filling the room near Ray Jr.'s casket.

Smokers migrated to the veranda, sending cigarette smoke swirling inside every time the doors opened. Mr. Allen didn't notice. He was snoring loudly in one of the veranda rocking chairs, walking stick across his lap like a weapon.

At two o'clock in the morning, Uncle Arthur announced that the funeral parlor was closing. "I'm tired. Marileigh and Ray Sr., are completely wrung out. Let's go home."

"But Arthur, that's not done," protested Miss Eula Napier, "You've always stayed open all night."

At that, Aunt Vinnie raised her voice. "Arthur and I are too old to stay here all night anymore and many of you are getting on in years, too. Let's all get to our beds!"

Marine Corporal Ray Anderson's visitation went down in Yuchi history as the last time Uncle Arthur's funeral parlor stayed open all night. Sadly, Ray Jr., wasn't the last young soldier from Yuchi to die in Vietnam. Those who followed Ray Jr., in death were honored just as he was, only this time Uncle Arthur opened the funeral parlor doors at 6:00 p.m. and locked up by 9:00 p.m.

When Every Day Was Halloween

The six months my family lived in a stucco duplex in a gloomy neighborhood on the south side of Birmingham was the scariest time of my life. The house was squeezed onto a small dark lot. Thorny overgrown bushes scratched the window screens at night. The creepy old house next door was so close I could have spit in its windows.

As a nine-year -old who had been uprooted from a cozy home not far from my grandparents, I was afraid of this aging neighborhood; I was terrified of the walk to our bleak new schoolhouse only a few blocks away, but our parents were excited to be leaving the steel mills of Birmingham for a new life in East Tennessee, where my daddy had landed a great new job.

I overheard my parents talking about the exciting new life we would have in East Tennessee and how lucky they were to find this duplex they could rent without a lease. "And we can move just as soon as you get your security clearance," said mother, cheerfully.

Even for 1950, the duplex was old-fashioned and smelled of coal ash from a furnace in the kitchen. An alley paved with cinders ran behind the house for the truck that delivered coal once a week. My younger brother Jim Boy didn't like the loud rumbling noise as the truck poured raw black coal down a chute into a rickety coal shed. Mrs. Davis, the grouchy widow who lived in the other side of the duplex, shared half the coal shed; I wondered why there was never anything but coal dust in the bin on her side. Daddy just laughed when he saw her sneaking a bucket of coal from our supply. "We won't be here for long. I don't mind sharing a few buckets of coal with the old girl."

Jim Boy and I shared a bedroom at the back of the duplex. We felt isolated back there next to the bathroom, so we whispered during the night. The sound of my brother's voice was comforting, even though he mostly whispered his fears about shadows that flitted across the half-dark room or noises from the street.

Our parents always listened to Edward R. Murrow's newscasts to get the latest news on the war in Korea; I couldn't help but overhear the famous newscaster's dramatic news about bloody battles and soldiers dying. I had nightmares about dead bodies and blazing big guns in that unknown foreign land.

I really tried to be the brave big sister for my younger brother. But it wasn't easy, especially at night when a shell-shocked neighbor began his nightly shrieks of hysterical laughing and crying. As this haunted World War II veteran relived the horrors of war, Jim and I cowered under our quilts, hoping the deranged young man didn't escape his room in the dark stone house so close to ours.

That was not all. Sometimes in the night we heard shuffling sounds coming from the coal shed just outside our bedroom window. Jim Boy whispered in the dark, "Do you hear it? Is he out there?"

"Oh no," I lied. "I think it's just a cat or the next-door neighbors' big dog. We're really safe in this room," I said. "We've got these steel burglar bars welded to our windows."

Jim Boy whispered, "But what if that mad man escapes and breaks in the side door? He could sneak down the hall and murder me and you in our beds!"

Nighttime was scary enough. But the daytime horror for me and Jim Boy was the frail old lady in the huge old house next door with every window shuttered. The only paint left on the rotting eaves was colorless and peeling. My brother and I called it the House of Horrors.

To make matters worse I heard her tell our mother that she was a spiritualist who called up the spirit of her late husband to comfort her in bed at night. Her wrinkled face looked like a dried apple and her bony body was always covered by a long floral bathrobe. We hid behind our porch railings to spy on her as she swept her porch.

Her name was Mrs. Gilman; one of our scariest days was the day she invited us inside her dark creepy house. Calling from her porch, she said, "Why don't you children ask your mother if you can come over? I've just made shortbread cookies that I think you'll like."

Cookies! That sounded good.

I suddenly lost my taste for cookies when she added in her creaky voice, "These cookies are my dead husband's favorite."

Winning is Everything

Bob was a happy man. He had just won a big victory at his church's vestry meeting. Bob liked to win. He liked the stunned look on the faces of people he had beaten, whether it was business, sports or the church.

Bob was sitting on his terrace, swirling the fine single malt Scotch in his glass. He liked to replay his victories once he got home. It was like winning twice. He chuckled to himself as he recalled how his sanctimonious priest Father Alan had suggested that the vestry discuss the issue of same gender marriage.

Bob was rather pleased with his performance. He had fired the first volley, loud and forceful, "We cannot allow two men to marry each other at St. Matthew's. It ain't gonna happen!" That was part of his strategy for winning.

"Calm down, Bob, let's have a civil discussion," said Greg. He was a giant of a man who coached football at the high school where Bob's son, Robby, was the star quarterback.

"Okay, okay, but we can't condone this kind of thing at St. Matthew's. It's not right," said Bob, a little more subdued, also part of his strategy.

Father Alan spoke up, "All of you know that we have gay members in our church. We allow them to be baptized, confirmed and take communion. Why exclude them from marriage?"

"Of course, gays are welcome here. But marriage is out of the question," asserted Bob, with a scowl directed at the other eight members of the vestry.

Then Jeff, a local plumbing contractor, said, "This issue is a no brainer for me. My son is gay. He grew up in this church. I'd like him to have the right to marry here."

Finally, Eugenie Barnstable weighed in. Shaking a gnarly finger in the direction of Father Alan, she snarled, "I am a charter member of this church and if this thing gets approved, you can say good-bye to my pledge plus the bequest in my will."

Then old Dr. Grant, who had delivered most of the babies in the community for many years, had his say, "I can't support same sex marriage in my church. I agree with Bob, it's not right."

Bob liked the old doctor and gave him an approving smile. The old guy had delivered Bob's son, the football star, and also his daughter, Emily, a National Merit Scholar, who was now a senior in college.

That's when Ashley, a stylish young matron, asked Dr. Grant if he had a reason for opposing gay marriage at St. Matthew's. "You bet I do. We will lose members and we will lose pledging units. We can't afford to be liberal," he said.

Finally, Marilyn, recreation director at the local YMCA, annoyed Bob greatly with her comment. He'd always been a little suspicious of her sexual orientation anyway. "I'd be surprised if everyone around this table doesn't have a gay relative or friend," said Marilyn. "I'd really like to see St. Matthew's welcome everyone with love and acceptance."

"Marilyn, you offend me greatly," shouted Mrs. Barnstable. "I can't think of anyone in my family who isn't perfectly normal."

"Same here," said Bob.

"Let's have the vote," said Father Alan.

"Who is for allowing same sex marriage at St. Matthew's?" Four hands were raised.

"All opposed?" Five hands shot up.

"Meeting adjourned," said Father Alan.

As Bob sat on his terrace following the meeting, he knew he had won again. He was a happy man.

When his mobile phone rang, he saw that the caller was Emily, his smart and wonderful daughter.

"Hi, Dad, I have some great news. I'm getting married!"

"Oh, sweetie, that's wonderful. Who's the lucky guy?"

After a long pause, Emily said, "Dad, her name is Susan. You will just love her!"

Baby Love

My mother never met a baby she didn't love. No infant escaped her baby radar. During a stroll in the shopping mall she could spot a baby the way some women zone in on a bargain. The baby could be in a stroller, a grocery cart or snuggled in a parent's arms. Babies, all babies, cute or plain, black, white or Asian, sensed the adoration of this petite little woman who spoke their secret language of coos, gurgles and smiles.

Some doting mothers appreciated her fascination with their babies. When my mother stopped a passing stroller to exclaim to the little passenger, "Aren't you just a little doll? You are just precious!" Those mothers beamed in agreement. *What a smart little woman. She obviously recognizes that my baby is exceptional.*

Not every passing parent was as pleased to have their offspring halted in the cereal aisle by my mother's attention. When the little lady stopped them to admire baby Ryan or tiny Suki, she sometimes got a scowl or frown from a parent who didn't know what to make of this baby-crazed matron. The parent might think, *Is this woman a baby snatcher? Is she for real?* Or maybe this may come from the germ-conscious mother*, I don't want this stranger breathing on my baby.*

She earned a few nasty looks at times when she stopped an unsuspecting parent on the street to offer unsolicited advice such as, "I hope you don't mind my saying so, but that baby needs some socks on those little feet." Or maybe Mother would add, "That baby needs a hat on his head. Those little ears are cold."

What made my mother love babies so much? I think it may be because she was the last child born into a family that already had six older children, three boys and three girls. All the older siblings adored baby Sadie who was born in 1916.

The family lived on a prosperous river valley farm on the Tennessee River near Guntersville, Alabama. The siblings all recalled that their little sister was cute, happy, and totally self-confident at an early age. With a mop of curly black hair, she charmed everyone she met. As an adult she was just under five feet tall, so she remained the baby sister.

One of my favorite anecdotes about my mother and babies took place in 1998 when she was already in her eighties, but still energetic and outgoing. We drove from our hometown in Tennessee to an employee picnic in Alabama, not far from Birmingham, where I was on a special assignment to help build employee morale at a construction site where communication was almost non-existent between the different crafts. Most of the skilled jobs were held by white employees. Most of the workers who did the heavy lifting were black. The racial divide was all too common in this part of Alabama, and my company found this bigotry unacceptable and non-productive. The picnic was to be a first step in solving the problem.

Mother and I arrived at the picnic site at a pleasant park built beside a man-made lake just out of town. The company had spared no expense on food, entertainment and door prizes, but the usual problem persisted. The black employees and their families sat on one side of the picnic pavilion while the white employees occupied the other side. My job was to take pictures, show enthusiasm, and get people talking to each other. It wasn't working.

It was my mother's love for babies that finally broke the ice. Unaware of the racial tension, she went around the divided groups talking to everyone. Her baby radar kicked in when she spotted a young black couple, the mother tenderly cuddling a baby boy while the doting daddy looked on with pride. Mother rushed over and began admiring the baby, who smiled and cooed at the attention of this little grandmotherly white lady.

"Please let me hold him," begged my mother. The baby's mother, unsure what to do, looked at the daddy for an answer. The daddy looked my mother up and down, then grinned, "Why, sure," he said.

Mother held the baby in her arms. "Aren't you just the cutest thing? You are just precious." The parents looked pleased, but still a little insecure, especially when my mother began to visit every table to show the little fellow off. "Look at this little angel," she said at every stop. "Have you ever seen such a happy little boy? Don't you just love him?"

At first it was the children, both black and white, who crowded around the baby. He laughed and giggled with joy at the children. Then the children's parents loosened up a little, several of the white women began talking to the baby's parents. Before long everyone began talking and laughing together. I never knew if the camaraderie transitioned to the job site, but I do know it was a start.

My mother died in 2011 just a few days short of her ninety-fifth birthday. I still treasure the picture I took of Mother, gently holding that adored little baby on the day the two of them worked a miracle.

Precious Memories

I've got stories rumbling around my jellied brain that I'm certainly enjoying while I wait to leave this old world behind. That baby-faced doctor says I'm in the last stages of dementia. Maybe so. I can't remember what I had for breakfast, but lots of sweet memories are streaming through my head like a picture show.

The folks who tip toe in this little room to see me here at the Shady Rest Old Folks Home think I've had a stroke. Wouldn't they be surprised to know I just don't want to be bothered? They'd croak if they knew I can hear every word they say. Like when that busy body Nancy Parker from my Golden Agers Sunday School class came by today. The old prune leaned over right in my face. "Don't Lula look plumb terrible? Wonder how long she's got?"

Eileen, my caregiver who's gonna be out of a job soon as I kick off, sighed, blowing her nose loud as a cow's fart. "I love Miss Lula dearly, but I don't think it'll be long now."

I guess that talk about dying got me thinking about my sweet mama and how she died of a terrible disease a few months before her fifty-sixth birthday. Only six years after we buried Mama, our family suffered another loss when the Tennessee Valley Authority took our land to build a huge new dam. Our farm and home are now just fond memories, buried beneath swirling waters of the lake that cover everything like Yankees invading Atlanta.

Today, in my fading mind I have been seeing a slideshow of my mama and papa, Sarey and Walter Bayer. Mama was a tiny woman with a gentle face like the picture of the mother of Jesus in our family Bible. I loved her dearly. Her passing left a hole in my heart deeper than the sinkhole out in the far pasture.

Up until she started losing weight and turning gray, I never saw her sit down. She cooked delicious meals on a wood stove in a kitchen hotter than the flames of hell, winter and summer. Every morning while the sky was still dark, Mama slipped into the kitchen, trying not to wake the family. First, she threw chunks of firewood on the glowing coals in the wood stove. While the fire was getting hot enough, Mama made biscuits, kneading flour, lard and buttermilk together with her bare hands. Lots of mornings, I slipped off the feather bed I shared with my older sister Alice. Barefoot in my nightshirt, I liked to watch as Mama boiled coffee in a big pot on top of the stove and baked dozens of fluffy biscuits so big they was called catheads.

One morning I was hanging too close to Mama as she lifted the boiling coffee pot off the fire. I bumped into her; hot coffee splashed all over my left arm leaving a blistering burn that lasted for months. I was rolling on the floor screaming in pain while Mama knelt beside me, crying and smearing my arm with butter to stop the burning. Folks back then used butter as a home remedy for burns. Turns out that cold water or ice was better medicine, but we didn't know that back then. Long after the accident, I bragged at school that the scar on my arm was made in the shape of Alabama and for a penny I'd let them touch it.

I'm getting worn out just thinking about all my mama did. She sewed all our clothes, even our underwear, on a pedal sewing machine. She and Lucy, the hired man's wife, washed our clothes in a big black wash pot over a hot wood fire in the yard. She canned and she cleaned. Best of all, she loved us, every one.

When she wasn't working at home, Mama drove the wagon to our little fieldstone church house out near the paved road to Huntsville. Mama took turns with her church lady friends, scrubbing and dusting every square inch before Sunday services. When it was Mama's turn to put flowers on the altar, she plucked blossoms from her flower garden that bloomed in colors like a rainbow all spring and summer.

Now my papa was another story. It wears me out just trying to tell anything he did besides eat, sleep and play checkers. He spent his days sitting on a bench in his general store, sometimes getting up to charge a sack of flour to a farm woman. He made more effort for the traveling salesmen that made stops at stores all along the river. I watched Papa shake their hands, eager to hear the news they picked up along their routes. They always paid cash for a good lunch of cheese that Papa sliced from an orange wheel of cheddar; they added a pack of saltines grabbed from the shelf behind the counter, and a big old green knobby pickle from the barrel.

When neighbor kids came in with a nickel to buy a cold soda pop, Papa didn't leave his bench. "Pick your drink over there in the cooler," he'd say, "and leave your money on the counter."

His beaky nose jutted out almost as far as the pipe that always hung from the corner of his mouth. Sometimes I thought his big nose was God's way of punishing him for being so mean to my brothers. He used them like slave labor on the farm, waking all three early every morning to milk the cows right at daybreak. After breakfast, he ordered the boys to the fields or the gardens, whatever needed tending. They hated him, especially Gordy, the oldest.

Sometimes Papa strolled around the barns and fields like an overseer thinking up new chores for the boys and the hired man to do. How did Papa spend his days? Mama joked, "Walter wears out the seat of his pants sitting on a bench in the store playing checkers."

That pipe seemed glued to his mouth; maybe that's why he never answered my questions. You should have seen him the time I asked about a curious thing I was seeing at the store. "Who are those ladies, Papa? They acting like they live here." He bit the pipe stem harder and didn't say nothing. Talking to Papa was like talking to the wall.

My Grandpa said, "Walter's got a bad case of the shut mouth. He don't talk unless he wants something. And his hearing ain't too good neither unless it's about money or 'what's for dinner?'"

If Mama had been looking for a handsome man when she married Papa, she needed her eyeglasses adjusted. I'm guessing he came over here from north Texas seeking his fortune in Blair County, Alabama, when the eligible ladies along the Red River rejected this scrawny fellow. Even I knew that women folk want a man who at least tries to win their hearts with flowers and sweet words. Papa was none of that. To his credit, he was tolerant when Mama's daddy came to live with us after Mamaw, our sweet granny, died. Grandpa Henry was headstrong; he liked to be the boss, but Papa never said nothing back to him.

When a couple of neighbor ladies spread a rumor that Papa was 'a cheating on Mama, I got the idea that he might be messing with them ladies I seen hanging around in back of the store. Some of 'em didn't look very nice. But I never said nothing to nobody about my suspicions.

I'm the baby of the family so I had more time with Mama than my half dozen older brothers and sisters. I was fifteen years old when Dr. John started coming out from town more often than usual. He'd been driving up the farm road in his horse and buggy for years checking on Grandpa Henry's sugar diabetes. But now he was seeing Mama, too, and nobody was telling me anything.

What's going on? I hung out in the hallway when Doc was in the house. I tried to listen in on my sisters whispering in the kitchen, but the whispering always stopped when I came around. I caught my brothers a couple of times on the front porch, their heads together, talking low. "You run on now, Lula," said my favorite brother, Hank. "This is man talk."

I watched Dr. John and my married sister Birdie help Mama to her bedroom, closing the door so all I could hear was mumbling. After Doc left, I asked my sister, "What's wrong with Mama? Does she have something awful like consumption?"

Looking melancholy, Birdie said, "Don't you worry, honey, Mama's just feeling a little poorly right now." I knew she was lying.

Where was my papa during these doctor visits? I'd heard my sisters complain that Papa took more interest in dumb cattle in the pasture than he did our mama. Mild-mannered Birdie actually raised her voice one day after he stomped in from the store for his dinner, never even asking about Mama before he started shoveling food down his gullet. "I'd think you'd ask how Mama's doing before you start cramming your face. She's getting worse every day."

Angrily pointing his fork at Birdie, Papa yelled, "Watch your mouth, girl. That's enough from you." Birdie hung her head, wiping tears; my sister didn't dare cross the old buzzard again.

Now, I was really curious. What did that mean?

I knew things were bad the day Doc drove his buggy to the store before heading back to the ferry. I ran barefoot down the dirt path to the store, rushing in the door before Doc got his horse hitched. I was leaning on the drink box hoping for a clue. That was sure a waste of time. Dr. John stalked over to the checkerboard, pointing a finger at Papa. "I need to talk to you, Walter."

Daddy scowled, "Doc, I can't leave my customers."

With a glance over his shoulder at me, Dr. John said, "Lula's right over there. She can take care of business for a few minutes. We need to talk about Sarey's condition."

Sarey's condition? I heard that part. But what was Sarey's condition? Papa and the doctor went off to the back room, so I couldn't listen in no more.

I ran from the store hoping Grandpa would tell me something. He was sitting as usual on the front porch in an old cane-bottom chair with his favorite yellow cat rubbing on the leg of his overalls. I loved my grandpa better than anything. I knew I was his favorite, maybe excepting for my cousin Marthey, who was named for our dead mamaw.

"Grandpa, what's all this whispering about Mama? Why's the doctor checking on both 'a you now? Don't you think I'm old enough to know something?"

With a frown as he stared out toward the river, Grandpa sighed, "Honey, your mama married beneath herself and now she's paying the price. I tried to tell her."

I knew Grandpa and Papa didn't like each other, but I never heard Grandpa say anything like that before. Everybody knew that Grandpa owned the farm, the house, and a lot of rental property besides. I figured Papa stayed at the store and out of Grandpa's way, only coming to the house at noon to eat a big dinner and to bed as soon as the sun set. Sometimes, he didn't come home at night. Said he was sitting up with his shotgun in the back room of the store 'cause he'd heard a gang of robbers was breaking into stores in these parts.

So what was Mama's condition? She was too old to be pregnant and way too young to die. Didn't her youngest daughter have a right to know? I was sure the other six knew.

My older sisters Mamie and Birdie started coming over to help with cooking and washing. Mamie, first in our family to drive a car, come by in the latest model of Henry Ford's boxy, black automobile to collect the washing, and took it to town to the Mill Village where a mill hand's wife was glad to make a few extra dollars.

My little mama was losing weight that she didn't have to lose. Her hair turned gray almost overnight; and it was getting so thin she was almost bald. I really got worried when she started going to bed during the day. That's when a visiting nurse in a starched white uniform and a cap like angel wings started driving up to the house in a big white van from the county health department. I couldn't figure what she was doing for Mama. Birdie carried hot water and towels to the bedroom, but I was shooed away.

By that time, I'd asked them all: Grandpa, the doctor, my sisters and my papa. "What's wrong with Mama?" All I got was a run around.

One day when the nurse was leaving, I stopped her just as she got to the van. "What's wrong with my mama?"

She didn't answer for a minute, just like everybody else. Then she said, "Sweetheart, I'm not supposed to say anything, but your mother has a female ailment. I'm so sorry."

Mama wasn't getting any better. I was getting scared. Finally, Dr. John called all seven of us kids to the parlor to tell us that our mama was dying. "She'll need full time care and bed rest until the end."

Birdie and Mamie cried. When I saw their tears, I started bawling, too. I heard Gordy, the oldest, mumble under his breath, "That son of a bitch!"

"Let me take care of Mama," I said. "I'll stay out of school."

My sister Birdie said, "Honey, you can't do that. You need to be in school."

But Dr. John overheard. "Wait a minute, Birdie. Let's talk about this. Lula still lives here. She's a smart young lady. She can fill in the gaps when you and Mamie and the nurse can't be here. She'll be a lot of company to Sarey."

Dr. John, looking serious, took me off to the dining room for what he called a private chat. "Lula, there's a few precautions you'll need to take if you help take care of your mama. I'll ask the nurse to come by and explain."

"I would do anything for my mama," I sobbed. "But I don't understand. Does she have a terrible disease like maybe cancer?"

For the first time in my life, I saw the doctor struggle for words. Finally he answered,

"Honey, your mama has what's called a venereal disease. You need to take extra precautions when you bathe and change her."

"No, no! That can't be right. My mama is a good woman."

The doctor frowned, taking a minute to find the right words. "This isn't the time to be mad at your papa, but I'm afraid she got it from him."

"Ain't there something you can do to save my mama?" Tears and snot were pouring down my face. Doc handed me his big white handkerchief.

"Lula, honey, I would give anything if I could help Sarey, but this disease is almost impossible to cure in women. It spreads to the female organs and then the bloodstream. Your mama is real sick." Doc took my hands in his; he looked about to join me in crying. "Honey, I'm so sorry."

Mama and I had lots of time together in those last days. Sometimes she asked me to slide her bed close to the window so she could see the river. "I shore love watching that old river roll by." I'm sort of glad she didn't live to see our home place covered up by the TVA's big lake.

The only good thing about those awful days were the visits from the public health nurse. She was so tender when she washed Mama and tender every time she found a place on that frail body to give Mama a shot. Thank goodness for anything that gave Mama a few hours peace from thrashing about. By now, Mama could barely talk, and she wasn't quite right in the head, but she did manage to whisper to this angel in white, "You a blessing."

Mama struggled to tell me what she wanted for her funeral. She begged me to get the church choir to sing her favorite hymn, "Precious Memories."

Mama left us on November 8, 1934. I'll always remember how she was grateful and loving, even in the agony of those last days. I'll never regret staying out of school to care for her.

So, here I am, ninety-four years old in an old-folks home, fuzzy brain and all. That baby-faced doctor was just here, stethoscope around his neck and a little computer thing in his hand. He shook his head and told Eileen, "There's little to no brain activity. Won't be long now."

Ha! That's what he thinks. Moving pictures of all those happy times spent with my mama are rolling around in my brain like a picture show. I ain't got space left to think about my sorry daddy. And I'm done being mad at TVA for taking our farm.

Hey, I see a shining angel floating my way. *Hello, Mama, is that you? I'm a coming!*

Lula Gets a Paddling

Sarey Bayer, mother of seven children, ages six to twenty-two, couldn't help but stand on the farmhouse porch, weeping as her youngest child, her precious six-year-old Lula, jumped aboard the family wagon headed for her first day of school. Lula was beaming as she turned back to wave good-bye to Mama. She didn't see Mama's tears. Lula was too excited. Hired man Rufus Harris, slapping the reins on the back of the family's sturdy mule, gave the command, "Away," and the wagon began rolling down the farm road, around the bend and out of Mama's sight.

Older sister Birdie, a recent graduate of Snead Seminary, shared the wagon seat with her baby sister. The year was 1922 and Lula was just starting school. Birdie, not quite twenty, was hired by the Marshall County school district to teach the community's youngsters at Baker's Chapel, the one-room schoolhouse that doubled as a Methodist meeting house on Sundays.

All the students loved their teacher, Miss Birdie, who patiently went through each day teaching reading, writing and ciphers to a roomful of youngsters from six to who knows how old. Most of her students were well behaved at school. They knew what awaited them at home if they either slacked in their lessons or didn't mind Miss Birdie.

Miss Birdie had one problem child, her little sister! Accustomed to being adored by her parents and older siblings, young Lula didn't think school rules applied to her. She talked when she should have been listening. Getting her lessons done was not a top priority. When Miss Birdie asked the class to line up for recess, Lula was always last to comply. In other words, Lula was a brat.

When all remedies failed to improve her baby sister's entitled behavior, Miss Birdie resorted to the paddle, but with a gentle hand; she only wanted to get her baby sister's attention. But little Lula howled and cried, "I'm gonna tell Mama on you."

As the wagon returned the teacher and her misbehaving sister to the farmhouse, the first one off the wagon was Lula, who ran to tell Mama about the paddling.

Mama wrapped protective arms around her cute little curly-haired Lula. When Birdie found the two huddled together in the kitchen, Mama's normally gentle demeanor changed to agitated mother hen. Before Birdie had a chance to say a word, Mama shook a finger at her older daughter, "Don't you dare paddle this baby ever again!"

Little Lula beamed in triumph at her older sister as Birdie quickly grasped that having her young sibling as a student just got a little harder.

Science Versus Aunt Cleo

My old neighborhood in Birmingham has changed so much I use the GPS on the rental car to get from the airport to my friend Glenda's house. I've only been away twelve years, but without the annoying voice on the GPS, I would be lost, and Glenda's house is still a few miles away.

Only a few more blocks and the manufactured voice on the GPS tells us, "You are approaching your destination." We stop in front of a neat frame house with metal chairs on the spacious front porch. My colleague, Josh Martin, in the passenger seat, asks if I am sure we are in the right place. Laughing, I say, "What's the matter, Josh, never been to a neighborhood like this?"

Josh reminds me that he's a Yankee. "I've never been south of the lab in my life." I warn him to be prepared for almost anything.

We park in front of the house where Glenda lives with her husband, Mitch, and their three youngsters. Mitch is football coach at our old high school; Glenda teaches gifted children at the neighborhood elementary school where she and I both learned to love books.

Josh is a microbiologist, and we are on a mission to do an environmental and genetic study of Glenda's birth family. I am excited, of course, to visit with my old friend, but eager to get started on my first real project for the lab.

An old Ford Crown Victoria is parked, partly in the driveway and partly on the sidewalk. The car's peeling vinyl roof looks familiar. And plastered on the car's rear window is a bumper sticker, "If it ain't King James, it ain't Bible." With those words, I know that the visitor could only be Glenda's dear Aunt Cleo.

At the slam of an aluminum screen door, Glenda and Aunt Cleo step onto the porch, both smiling. A little boy, maybe about three, peeps out from behind Glenda as she idly runs her fingers through his coarse black hair. The child's hair is eerily like his late grandfather Guy's hair.

My friend hasn't changed much in the years since our last visit. Still dark-haired and pretty, she has an arm around tiny Aunt Cleo, who only comes to Glenda's shoulder. But Aunt Cleo looks taller because of the hair piled like stacks of pancakes on top of her head. She told me long ago that women in her church don't cut their hair. "If a woman has long hair, it is a glory to her and to God," she said.

Glenda and I grew up enjoying Aunt Cleo's visits. When she drove down the winding highway from her home on Sand Mountain, she always brought a coconut cake to share and a big bowl of field peas from her garden. Aunt Cleo worried a lot about Glenda's parents, Oleta and Guy. Although it did no good at all, older sister Cleo lectured her sister Oleta on the evils of strong drink. On every visit, Aunt Cleo cleaned her sister's messy house as best she could. Oleta's husband Guy just stayed outside, drinking moonshine and working on his old car until Aunt Cleo went to bed.

Glenda and I loved visiting Aunt Cleo's little farm on the mountain for a few weeks every summer. We sat with her on the front porch, shelling peas and listening to her stories. The only thing we didn't enjoy was going to Aunt Cleo's Sanctification church on Sundays. Preacher Buford shouted from the pulpit. Sometimes he scared me talking about sins I never thought about committing, like fornication and idolatry. I hoped I would never do those things because I didn't want to go to his fiery hell.

When I see Aunt Cleo on the porch with Glenda, she is just exactly as I remember, the piles of long, gray hair, wearing the usual outfit favored by women in her church, a long-sleeved blouse and long denim skirt reaching to the tops of her sensible shoes. "Come in this house," shouts Aunt Cleo, motioning us up the steps. I can see the feisty little lady is already taking over.

On the porch, Aunt Cleo hugs me so hard I lose my breath. Glenda welcomes me with a huge hug, but not as painful. Josh just stands there awkwardly.

Finally, Aunt Cleo spots Josh. "Is this good-looking man your husband?" she asks with a wink.

Blushing, I explain that Josh and I work together. "Josh, I'd like you to meet Aunt Cleo."

He steps forward to shake her hand. Then she makes the situation worse. "Come here, young man, and give Aunt Cleo a hug." He hugs her stiffly, shooting me a puzzled look.

Once we get inside, Glenda invites us all to sit in the living room. Aunt Cleo claims a tiny rocker just her size. Josh takes a chair in the corner, out of the way of the women. The little boy grabs a plastic toy from the sofa and runs out of the room. I can hear his dad, Mitch, and the other two kids playing a game in a back room of the house. Glenda and I sit together on the sofa, where she looks a little uncomfortable. We are both happy to see Aunt Cleo, but I suspect she's wondering how Aunt Cleo's presence will affect our plans.

I asked Aunt Cleo if Glenda told her about my new job at Pine Valley National Lab. "No, honey, she just said you were coming and I wanted to see you. I've missed you girls since you've got all grown up."

Glenda finally speaks up. "We're really proud of Gloria. She just got her doctorate in genetics and a great new job as a researcher at the lab."

"That's real good, honey. But what in the world is genetics?" With a nod to Josh, I ask him to explain genetics to Aunt Cleo. His glare tells me our collaboration on this project has already hit a rough spot.

The little lady turns her chair toward Josh, not wanting to miss a word. "Every human has millions of genes in their bodies." Josh uses a finger, drawing a long curving chain in the air. "These genes link together in thousands of different ways to determine characteristics and behaviors," he explains.

Aunt Cleo nods. "I'm listening," she says.

"For example, a parent with red hair and blue eyes might have one or more children with red hair and blue eyes. More recent studies are showing the possibility that genes might contribute to a person's intelligence or perhaps even alcoholism or suicide."

Aunt Cleo shakes her head, "I hear what you are saying, young man, but I disagree! Only God can give a baby its eye and hair color. And the same God makes people behave or misbehave according to his plan."

"Yes, ma'am," says Josh, "but it is God who made our bodies and the chemistry inside us that makes us who we are."

"Okay, go on."

"So, Gloria went to college for a long time and got an advanced degree in genetics. That's the branch of biology that deals with heredity and variations of organisms." Getting into his subject, he describes how I can use my training to learn more about changes in genes or mutations in genes that might determine disease or birth defects. "In our lab, we are mostly interested in the effects of radiation on genes. But we know that Glenda's daddy, Guy, worked in underground mines for most of his life and those mines are filled with radon gas, a type of radiation."

Looking directly at me and Glenda, who are listening intently on the sofa, he finishes up by telling Aunt Cleo that my work is very important in preventing disease or even developing medications that help people with high blood pressure, heart disease or even cancer.

So why are you visiting my sweet Glenda? What's she got to do with genetic studies?

I answer her question because I am expecting the explosion that I got. "Josh and I are here to do an environmental and genetic study of what made your sister Oleta and her husband Guy drink themselves to death. There's no doubt they were alcoholics. And what made their son, Duane, fight so much? And then eventually take his own life?" Aunt Cleo is frowning before I finish.

"But the best part of the study has to do with Glenda. Did she inherit her intelligence? Did she inherit her confidence? What made her the successful person that she is?"

"I know the answers to all that and I didn't even go to college," said Aunt Cleo.

Trying to get in the last word, I told her that Josh and I have a good feeling that our studies of Glenda's family will add greatly to a better understanding of what makes some people alcoholics and some people exceptionally competent like Glenda.

Turning away from Josh, Aunt Cleo glares at her niece. "Glenda, did you agree to this?"

Meekly, she says, "Yes ma'am, I did. I think if I know more about what made Mama and Daddy drink like they did, it might help me raise my kids a different way. And every time my kids fight, I wonder if they'll turn out like Duane."

The old lady puffs up like a toad, pointing an arthritic finger toward each of us in the room. "What you are planning to do is an abomination!" she screeches in a tone reminding me of Preacher Buford. "The Lord made us and we are not to interfere with his handiwork. You don't need blood tests and those samples that you talked about. I can tell you exactly what made your parents drink like fools and ruin their lives," she said, only slightly calmer.

"Your mama was a wild little thing all her growing up years. She worried me to death when she got older, running after boys and dressing like a tramp. Why, she couldn't wait to get off the mountain and find her a man. Our mama cried her eyes out over that girl. And we all prayed until we couldn't pray no more."

"Then what does she do? She slips off to Birmingham on the early morning bus off the mountain and marries the first man that looks twice at her. And him a foreigner that barely speaks English. Her a mountain girl and him from across the ocean. You can forget your genetics. The two of them never knowed each other. He didn't know what he had got into and Oleta didn't understand him at all. So the only thing they could do together was to drink and have sex."

"I see your point," I said. Glenda looks embarrassed. Aunt Cleo keeps going.

"And about Duane. The only person that ever loved that boy was Glenda. And that ain't what he wanted. He wanted his mama and his daddy to love him. By the time he come along, Guy and Oleta didn't love nothing but the bottle. I tried to love him, but he wouldn't let me. Then he took to drinking when he was still young and that muddled his brain to the point that he didn't know right from wrong."

"When he killed hisself, he killed a part of me and his sister, too. We'll never get over it." She pulls a rumpled tissue from her sleeve and dabs at her tears.

Glenda fidgets on the sofa. Between sobs, Glenda tells us that Duane's death is the worst thing that's ever happened. "I feel so guilty that I couldn't help him."

Josh finally breaks the long silence. "Aunt Cleo, do you have any thoughts on why Glenda has turned out so well?"

"Some babies are just born happy and sweet and she was that kind of baby. We all loved her. Even Guy and Oleta was able to love her. When her parents went off the deep end, I watched this precious little girl become the mommy to the whole family," she said, still wiping her tears.

"Then Gloria and her family moved across the street and Glenda had a friend she could talk to. Gloria's sweet mother helped her with things that girls need as they grow up. But best of all, Gloria and Glenda went to church and grew up in the Lord's house. It was in that church that Glenda met Mitch, the God-fearing man she married. It was the will of God, not genetics, that made our Glenda believe in herself and turn out to be so smart."

With that, Aunt Cleo looked around the room. "Well, that's all I have to say. I hope I'm not too disagreeable."

Josh is smiling now. "No, ma'am, you're not disagreeable. You answered our questions about Glenda's family background before we even asked. That's the important nurture part of our study. Thank you so much."

"I like you, young man. I disagree with this genetic study business, but I appreciate your talking to me about it."

Then I explain that the nature part of our study involves just a few more things like taking a look at family medical records and getting a DNA sample from Glenda. And I'll ask Glenda if she might have a hairbrush or some clothes that might give us a biological sample from her parents or her brother.

"You don't need to do another thing," she shouts, with a passion usually reserved for church. "God is still in charge!"

Josh looks bewildered. I try to guide the conversation back to our mission.

"Aunt Cleo, I want you to know that going off to college and studying genetics did not change my belief in God. But I truly believe that God gives each of us gifts that we use to help ourselves and others."

"Maybe so," she said. "I'll have to do some praying about this."

She gets up from the rocking chair. "I'm going back to hug those babies and Mitch before I head back up the mountain. Y'all come see me," she says.

"I'd like to," says Josh.

Turning to me, he says, "Gloria, let's do that."

Before she leaves the room, Aunt Cleo whispers in my ear. "I like that young man. Looks like good husband material to me."

Papa Buys a Model A

Sometime back before the Great Depression laid the country low, folks out in Henryville were still driving wagons pulled by sturdy mules. On our farm, not only did we have a mule and a farm wagon, but also, my grandpa had a fine buggy and a high-stepping horse.

But all that changed around 1929 when Papa heard that a barge load of brand-new Model A Fords had just been unloaded across the river in Starnesville. Papa got the big idea to buy one. He broke the news at the breakfast table one morning after smearing the last bits of fried egg and sausage off his plate with a bite of biscuit. "Yep, I'm going into town this morning and buying me a motor car."

"Walter, don't we need to talk about this? That's a lot a money," said Mama, as she began clearing the table, picking up plates and coffee cups.

"Hell, no, Sarey, I been needing me a motor car for a long time."

Grandpa just outright told him, "Walt, before you get you a automobile, there's lots that needs a doing on this farm."

"We got everything we need on this farm. Ain't no reason why I can't get me a motor car," Papa shouted.

Grandpa just rolled his eyes. Mama muttered under her breath. "Lord, help us."

"Next time you all see me, I'll be driving me a brand-new Ford," said Papa as he loudly scooted his chair back from the table and headed for the barn.

Grandpa and I followed him. Rufus the hired man was already outside the barn door harnessing up the mule.

Grandpa let go a big wad of chewing tobacco which nearly landed on my papa's brogans. "Since when did you learn to drive, Walter Bayer?" Grandpa shouted.

Turning red in the face, Papa shouted back, "It can't be that hard to drive. Lots a them folks in town are driving and they ain't no smarter than me."

"Take me, Papa, take me," I begged. As the last of seven young 'uns left at home, I never wanted to miss a trip to town. Besides, it was a hot summer day, and I was hoping Papa might buy me a nice cold Co-Cola from the drink box at the ferry landing. Papa was already popping the leather reins on our old mule's back when he finally said the words I wanted to hear. "Hop in Lula. Set on the wagon bed behind me and Rufus."

My bare feet on the hot boards were burning like I'd stepped on an ant hill. Plus, I was wishing for my sun bonnet to shade my face. But I kept my mouth shut. Papa didn't have anything on his mind except buying a motor car.

When we got down to the ferry landing, a whole bunch of our neighbors were waiting to cross the river, some in wagons loaded with fresh corn and green beans to sell in town. The salesman that called on Papa's store shouted from his nice buggy, "Howdy, Mr. Walter." Papa just nodded, jostling our wagon to get a good place in line.

All the way across the river our old mule stomped and brayed and pounded the ferry bottom like the rumble of thunder. Finally, on the town side, Papa whacked that mule on the rump and off we rolled up the side road toward Starnes Avenue where those brand-new motor cars were waiting. I knew Papa would about die if those city folks bought 'em all before he got there.

I'd never seen a motor car in all my thirteen years. From my seat in the back of the wagon, all I could see was a shiny box of a thing held up by four wagon wheels. Looked like maybe the wheels were wrapped in rubber.

"Lordy, Lordy," said Papa, when he got his first look at those Model A's all in a row in front of Mr. Purdy's hardware store. "Ain't they a sight to behold!"

"They sho are fine, Mr. Walter. Yes suh," said Rufus.

Papa stared reverently at those new motor cars as if God had delivered one just for Walter Bayer. Despite the heat of the afternoon sun, town men in suits, shiny shoes, and their summer straw fedoras were kicking the tires and looking for price tags. Men from the country were hanging back, some fanning with their work hats, but curious just the same.

Before he had time to change his mind, Papa jumped off the wagon looking for a salesman. Only a few minutes later, Papa handed over $500 dollars in cash money to a skinny salesman in a baggy striped suit. "You bought the first one today, Mr. Bayer," he quipped.

That's when the salesman invited Papa to climb on board for a driving lesson. I watched as Papa sneered at the milling crowd as if he were the King of Egypt, everyone gawking as my proud Papa took the wheel.

Rufus and I, standing at the back of the crowd, were embarrassed for Papa when the new vehicle jerked and quivered before he got it rolling. A few of the onlookers laughed out loud. He finally got the Ford going for a short drive around the block and arrived back at the starting point with brakes squealing and the salesman making a quick exit.

"Come on, Lula, let's head for home," Papa called.

"Papa, don't you think you need a little more driving practice before we cross the river?" His hateful stare told me not to say another word.

"Get in here, girl! I'm gonna show the folks in Henryville that Walter Bayer ain't driving a mule no more."

I climbed aboard, sorta wishing I was riding back with Rufus in the wagon. But I didn't want to make Papa any madder. After a few groans from the engine, he finally drove the few blocks to the ferry without another problem.

Papa's new Model A was the only motor car in line to board the ferry. Barefoot boys ran over to gawk; a few touched the shiny black fenders, making sure it wasn't just a mirage stirred up by the hot summer sun. Some of our neighbors waved from their wagons, "Hey Walter, what you got there?" Papa was beaming.

Finally, the ferry man motioned for us to board. I thought everything was going well until the Ford kept on rolling, closer and closer to the end of the ferry. Wasn't much between us and hitting the river head on. In his panic, Papa didn't stomp the brakes hard enough. I knew we were in trouble when he started yelling, "Whoa, whoa, you son of a bitch!"

About that time, the front wheel on the passenger side dropped off the side of the ferry. Hanging there, my face was almost touching the swirling water. I commenced to praying, *Jesus, dear Jesus, please don't let me drown.*

Papa was yelling, the horses and mules were squealing. Thank God for the ferry man and his helper. In all the uproar, those two came to my rescue. With one at the front bumper and the other at the back, those brawny men lifted the Ford as if it were a crate of squawking chickens and plopped it back on deck.

Sadly, I knew that the tale of Papa's mishap on the ferry had more than likely reached Henryville before we got home. A good story gets around in a hurry, especially if the joke is on somebody else.

By the time we arrived back at the farm, Grandpa Henry was down at the barn, just waiting. "Well, Walter, I see you got that automobile." I could tell he was trying hard not to laugh. "I hear you nearly ran the thang off the ferry."

Papa was so mad, he shouted, "Who told you that?"

"Walter, you know I'm just having a little fun with you," said Grandpa. "You got your automobile. Enjoy it."

Next thing I knew, my brother Johnny, red in the face from the heat, still carrying his hoe from weeding the vegetable garden, came a running from back of the house, yelling, "Oh, man, I love it. Take me for a ride, Papa. Please!"

"Hop in, son, where you want to go?" I watched as the two drove out of sight, Papa was sitting up straight and tall at the wheel. Johnny was leaning his head back and laughing with pure joy.

Grandpa shook his head in wonder as the disappearing Model A stirred up a cloud of dust. "I'm here to tell you that thang will never replace a good horse," he declared.

The Tricycle

The dinette table in Aunt Dee's kitchen was full of all my favorite food, steam still coming off the big bowl of black-eyed peas. A lump of fatback the size of a doorknob oozed good old hog grease to flavor the peas. When Aunt Dee set the iron skillet of brown-crusty cornbread on a hot pad right in front of me, I wanted to grab a hunk and slather it with butter right that minute.

A smiling Aunt Dee read my mind, "No, Jim Boy, you can't touch the cornbread till your Uncle Bud gets here. This is his dinner break."

I looked around the kitchen, still hot from the oven. The room was filled with good smells, like the crispy fried okra that was better than popcorn. In the summer heat my legs were sticking to the red plastic covering on the dinette chair, but I didn't care. I loved being at Aunt Dee's house on the farm.

She told us that morning as she stood at the stove, peas in the pot, potatoes boiling, "After we eat, we'll walk down to the creek and wade. Would you like that?"

"Oh yay," I shouted. "Yes, yes!"

My sister Janis, in her flowered sundress and with her hands tucked under her bottom to keep from grabbing a spoonful of fluffy mashed potatoes, sat across from me. "I love your mashed potatoes, Aunt Dee. Why don't you teach our mama to cook like you do?" Our favorite aunt just smiled.

Squirming on the sticky chair seat, I said to no one in particular, "Hurry up, Uncle Bud, I'm dying of hunger!" My sister and Aunt Dee both laughed.

"I think I hear him now," said Aunt Dee. Then the front door slammed, the sound of his boots clomped on the pine floor.

Uncle Bud laid his Stetson hat and a big pistol on the sink counter, the odor of cigar wiping out the good smell of food with fumes that made my eyes water. Rings of sweat circled the arm holes of his tan deputy sheriff's uniform. His big silver badge flashed as he clomped to the table. He pulled out a chair so hard that the chrome legs slid from under the table with a loud thump.

"Hey, y'all," he said, grabbing a plate. "Dee, pour me some of that buttermilk."

Aunt Dee jumped up from her seat at the table, hurrying to get her husband the buttermilk he demanded. "Let's eat," he said in his booming voice.

Why didn't he say "please" to Aunt Dee? Why didn't we bless our food before we ate? Our mama had some rules. The big man at the table sort of scared me, so I didn't say anything. Janis, not sure what to do, waited a minute, then grabbed the bowl of mashed potatoes.

"Bud, we had a letter from Buddy today. Now the war's over the Marines will be sending him back to the states. I've worried myself sick about him being in the thick of fighting over in the Philippines."

"That's good," he said. "We need the boy back on the farm."

"What kind of morning you been having?" asked Aunt Dee.

Waving his fork in excitement, Uncle Bud said, "I wish you could have seen that nigger I knocked off a coal truck this morning. I told that nigger he didn't have no business up there. Nigger just cowered down and didn't move."

"Was he trying to catch a ride?" asked Aunt Dee.

"Hell, no, I'm pretty sure the bastard was stealing coal. I knocked the shit out of him with my billy stick."

"Bud, maybe we don't need to talk about this anymore in front of the kids."

"They're old enough to learn what it's like out there," he bellowed. "When I got back in my cruiser, he was still a laying there in the gravel beside the truck, nigger blood all over his nappy head."

Uncle Bud seemed satisfied that his morning had gone so well. He drank his buttermilk in big gulps and shoveled Aunt Dee's good food in his mouth, chomping loudly. Our mama would have made him leave the table.

Janis stopped eating, turning pale. I couldn't take another bite either.

Wiping his empty plate with the last bit of corn bread, Uncle Bud noticed that Janis and I didn't eat very much. "What's wrong with you kids? If you don't start eating, we'll have to feed you to the hogs."

Both of us looked to Aunt Dee, hoping she'd protect us. But she just sat there.

When Uncle Bud scooted his chair back and got up to leave, he stuffed the big pistol back in the holster on his belt. I could see greasy stains on the head band of his hat as he slammed it on his head.

If I was upset about the ugly things he said at the table, my day was about to get worse.

"Come on, boy, I want you to ride in the cruiser with me this afternoon. I'll show you what it's like to be a deputy sheriff."

Screwing up my courage, I said, "I can't go today. Aunt Dee is taking us to the creek to wade."

"She can take you tomorrow, boy. Go pee and let's get going."

I looked to my aunt and my sister for help. They just looked blank. Guess they're afraid of him, too. Hanging my head, I followed him to the cruiser.

He drove for a while on county roads I'd never been on before. His police radio buzzed with static. A couple of times, I heard gravel ping under the cruiser. The smoke from his cigar was making me feel sick, but I was afraid to say anything.

Finally, Uncle Bud said, "What's a matter with you, boy? Cat got your tongue?"

"My name is Jim," I whispered.

"What's that you said?"

Louder, I said, "My name is Jim."

"I know your name, boy!"

When a garbled voice came over the radio, Uncle Bud picked up the microphone to respond. "Roger, I'm on my way."

"Hey, I got a call to make. This old nigger woman passed a bad check. We'll go shake her up a little."

He seemed almost happy when he parked the cruiser in front of a run-down old house with a sagging porch. "Open up, this is the law," he shouted. A thin little dark-skinned woman peeped out the door in answer to his loud banging.

Uncle Bud berated the woman, waving his pistol in the air. I could see her crying, trying to explain that she'd take the money to the bank just as soon as her son got off work. I heard her say she was sorry. It was just a mistake. But he kept on yelling.

I couldn't stand it any longer. Getting out of the cruiser, I yelled, "Stop it, Uncle Bud, just stop it!"

Uncle Bud, red in the face, screamed. "Get back in the car, boy! Right now!"

He was so mad, he drove away in a rush, spewing mud and gravel as he turned around in the dirt yard.

He didn't say anything for a long time. Maybe he felt bad about the scene I witnessed. I don't know. Then he turned to me, "Hey, boy, I'm gonna take you to the hardware store and buy you a tricycle. You'd like that, wouldn't you?"

"I guess so."

When my daddy came to the farm a few days later to take me and Janis back to the city, he loaded the big red tricycle in the car trunk. "That's really a nice tricycle," he said.

I didn't say anything. But Janis talked for twenty miles about the dogs, the horse and wading in the creek. "We had so much fun," she said. Then she added, "when Uncle Bud wasn't there."

Daddy just nodded.

I ran to Mama for a hug when we got back to our little house on Wilson Road in Birmingham. "How's my little man?" she said with a huge smile. "I hear Uncle Bud bought you a nice big tricycle."

"I hate that tricycle," I said.

"Jim Boy, you know our rule. We don't say we hate anything. You can say you don't like something, but never ever use the word hate."

"I'm sorry, Mama, but I really, really HATE that tricycle."

The Thirty-Year War

The troop transport plane landed at the military airbase in Vietnam on the blackest, most fearful night of my life. The minute my boots touched the tarmac, I breathed hot humid air heavy with an unnatural smell that was both sweet and spicy mixed with the rancid odor of unwashed bodies. This was my welcome to Vietnam; I smelled and tasted that smell day and night for the next thirteen months.

Sometimes when our company skirmished with the almost invisible enemy hidden in the jungles, the scent got lost in the odor of gunpowder belched from mortar shells and fired from tanks crashing through thick foliage. Sometimes fire and smoke blazed from the M-16 rifles of the infantry that protected me and my buddies as we were digging ditches and laying cable so the 11th Light Infantry of the Americale Division could send communications from one rotting jungle skirmish to the other.

When the choppers came in bringing us more cable or picking up the wounded and the dead, the odor of aircraft fuel blanketed the area until lift-off to base camp. The popping sound of the rotor blades thrashing the hot humid air sounded like Mama back home in Alabama standing on the back door step shaking the hell out of a dusty rug. Home seemed a lifetime away.

God, I missed Mama. She'd have been glad to know I had a little buddy over here to help me get through this stinking war. Little Bit and I met during lineman school in Fort Gordon, Georgia. Little Bit was eighteen, a skinny boy from Mississippi.

Sometimes he joked about being so small. "You should a seen that recruiting sergeant in Tupelo holding his breath till I stepped on the scale. I barely made the weight limit," he grinned.

I was nineteen, a little bigger, but not much. I joined the Army at the suggestion of the judge back home in Selma. "Tommy, I'll overlook this latest arrest for fighting if you'll join the Army and get out of town for a while."

Everybody liked Little Bit. Me, I couldn't keep out of cuss fights, and I sometimes threw a punch or two if somebody pissed me off. Living like we did wore me down. Ten of us lived in a tent structure with a wooden floor. The dwelling was called a hooch. We were slammed into bunks with no space to call our own. We couldn't do anything but sleep in our bunks because it was too damn hot and too damn dark. Rats were everywhere. They could even smell food in a can of C-rations. God, it was miserable.

We were all over Nam following Americale. When I wasn't laying cable and setting up communications, I was doing guard duty. One night in Phu Bai, on my first night on guard, the lieutenant told me, "Watch out for sappers, they'll try to sneak in our camp."

I knew what he meant about sappers. They were Viet Cong who tried to creep inside the compound with orders to plant explosives or to kill as many soldiers as they could. When one got in camp, no one rested until we caught the bastard. Nobody wants a sapper getting through on their watch. I was feeling as tight as a string on a cheap banjo.

I was at my post overlooking the garbage dump when I heard a familiar rustling that reminded me of deer slipping through the woods, sounds like I'd heard on my deer stand at Big Creek back home. But that Nam smell suffocated all thoughts of home. I listened, beads of sweat on my upper lip, my hands sweating on my rifle stock. The sound was like squirrels swishing through oak trees or foxes weaving through sage grass. Only trouble is there ain't no oak trees or sage grass in Nam, not around Phu Bai. I couldn't see nothing or nobody, except the rats making their rounds in the bunker.

After my watch I went back to the hooch. I whispered to Bit, "You can't imagine what it's like out there. I was scared to death."

"Next time, I'll go with you," he whispered. We both knew the lieutenant wouldn't go for no buddy deals on guard duty. But we did it anyway.

Next night was Bit's turn. I slipped out, making my way through the sleeping camp to that same old bunker overlooking the garbage dump. "Hey, buddy," I whispered, crawling into the damp bunker, scattering the rats, and jarring my nerves.

"Look out there," hissed Bit. "Look out there!"

In the dimness, I could see small children prowling around on the garbage dump, digging with their hands for potato peelings or anything they could scavenge. They might be Cong in the morning, but tonight they were just starving people.

The next afternoon, we had some leave and I said, "Bit, let's go into town."

"Okay," he said, "don't forget the lieutenant said don't get caught there after dark."

Calling Phu Bai a town was like calling Cam Ranh Bay a tropical resort. It was a pitiful collection of filthy streets and ramshackle buildings. But Bit and I found the bar and stepped into the dim, musty room; the Nam smell was stronger than ever.

A sour vomit taste welled up in my throat, but, hell, I was on leave. I gagged it back and ordered a beer, and then another. A couple of other GIs were there so Bit and I swapped a few jokes with them, mostly about how horny we were.

One of the guys, a tall, red-headed dude from Georgia, was flirting with a local whore. She looked about fourteen, but she was selling and he was buying. The bartender watched but didn't say anything. When it was about dark, Little Bit said, "Tommy, we got to go."

"I'm not going nowhere," I swore. Enough beers and I didn't care what the lieutenant said.

Little Bit puffed up, all five foot four of him, and he yelled at me. "If you don't come right now, I'm going to beat the shit out of you."

I nearly fell off the bar stool laughing at the little tough guy, but I left.

The next morning on the sandy road in front of our compound, the MPs found the bodies of two GIs, throats slit and blood everywhere. We all went out and looked, horrified, while the Medics took the bodies away. One of the dead guys was the redhead we'd seen at the bar. I wonder what the Army told his next of kin.

Some of the worst fighting for the Americale was in the central highlands. We'd been hearing talk about body count; it got personal when the lieutenant told us, "Boys, we're going out there in the morning."

I was so scared I couldn't stop shaking. My bunk shook from my trembling, making drumming noises on the wooden floor. The other guys bitched at me during that long night. Next morning, the truck came to get us. I told Little Bit, "I can't go."

"Yes, you can, Buddy. We'll just dig those ditches on our bellies." He hugged me, right there in the hooch. And I'm not a queer, not then and not now. But I hugged him back and we went out and got on the truck.

What happened after that is something I cannot talk about to this day. The fighting was so fierce and so bloody you would not want to hear the details. I still have nightmares about it. Sometimes, when I kill a deer and field dress it out in the woods, the smell of warm blood and the guts laying there in the leaves makes me gag with the memory.

Vietnam was rough duty. Maybe the worst of it was when Little Bit got the message from home. His Daddy had died of a heart attack. The Army gave him thirty-days of compassionate leave; Little Bit packed his duffel and boarded a transport out of Nam. I knew I'd never see him again. I was sure I was going to die out there all alone.

Thirty days later, I had just got back from the mess tent when Little Bit walks up with a big grin on his face. I had forgotten how young he looked, face innocent as a baby. I was so mad at him for coming back, but I was sure glad to see him. I yelled in his face, "Little Buddy, why did you come back here? You know the Army wouldn't have made you come back to this hell hole."

"Well, I didn't want you to finish the war all alone," he answered.

We did finish our part of the war, and in September of 1969, they put us on a transport and flew us back to the States. I told Little Bit good-bye in the Atlanta airport. "I'm gonna get married around Christmas. I want you to be my best man."

"I'll be there," he promised.

Well, after that, I went a little crazy. I had eleven months left in my enlistment and they sent me to Fort Jackson, South Carolina. I stayed drunk most of the time and acted like a complete shit, whether I was sober or drunk. My girlfriend back home in Selma agreed to go ahead and marry me, but I'll never know why. I was surely no prize. I sent a message to Little Bit out at Fort Gordon, Kansas, where he was finishing his enlistment. "We are looking for you in Selma, Alabama, on December 22 for a wedding," read the message.

I never heard a word. On the day before the wedding my daddy asked me, "Son, that boy ain't gonna show, is he?"

"I guess not," I shrugged, like I didn't care. Daddy was my best man.

After I got out of the Army, I got into the ironworker trade, working at power plant construction sites all over the country. Construction sites were the best places for me because I still had some of the bad boy in me. I was hard to get along with, getting into scraps here and there. It was good that I could move on whenever I wore out my welcome.

I didn't think about Little Bit all the time, but when something reminded me of Vietnam, I thought about him and wondered where he was. I'd like to see my little buddy.

I was so hard to get along with that my first wife took the kids and left after about ten years. I don't blame her, really, but I missed the kids badly. The two of us should never have got married in the first place considering the state I was in after Vietnam. The Army counselor told me, "A lot of guys have gone a little wild after being over there."

He told me out of three million troops that did time in Nam, more than five hundred thousand suffered from PTSD, divorce, suicide, drug addiction and alcohol addiction. I felt like a total jerk for being on that list. I told myself that Little Bit wouldn't have been that stupid.

After my divorce I went looking for Little Bit. I checked the Wall to make sure his name wasn't on it. I'd had a thought that maybe he'd reenlisted and got sent back over there. But his name wasn't on the Wall. I went to Veteran's Day events every year, hoping I'd see him. But maybe he'd got a big dose of me in Vietnam. Maybe he didn't want to have anything to do with me anymore.

I finally got squared away enough that I met a nice woman in Louisiana. Lisa and I lived together for a little while and finally got married. I was real tickled that my kids came to the wedding. I told Lisa a few things about Vietnam and how I'd like to find my old buddy.

I showed her a picture of the two of us sitting in the doorway of the hooch. I'd written on back of the picture, "Phu Bai,

November 28, 1968." Little Bit had his shirt off, showing his narrow shoulders and chest like a bird. I had on my khaki T-shirt, dog tags dangling from my neck. I knew I was sweating. I always did.

Lisa studied the picture. "You both look like children," she said, "but your friend looks like a sweet, innocent puppy."

"Why do you want to find him so bad?" she asked me one day after I'd been going through phone books from Mississippi trying to find a listing for Little Bit. His real name was Earl Martin and I was excited that I'd found a listing in Houston, Mississippi, for an Early Martin.

Not too long after that, Lisa and I drove over to Tupelo, Little Bit's hometown. I asked at the Lee County Courthouse for any sign of an Earl Martin. He didn't own property there and didn't have a Mississippi driver's license. There was no trace of Little Bit.

Lisa said, "Well, Houston is only thirty-six miles from Tupelo. Why don't we drive down and check out this Early Martin?"

I didn't want to call the number and be disappointed, so we just drove down to Houston and found the street where Early Martin lived. I was so anxious I was sick to my stomach. Lisa asked, "Do you want me to go to the door?"

I watched as a large black woman came to the door. I could hear her voice from the car. "Lord, honey, I wish I could help you, but I'm Early Martin, and I ain't never been to Vietnam.

Lisa and I had a good laugh. It felt good to laugh that day. If I ever did find Little Bit, I planned to tell him about his almost namesake in Mississippi.

The next year I was working in Decatur, Alabama. *The News-Herald* had an article saying the Travelling Wall Exhibit was going to be in Birmingham with a display of Vietnam-era equipment. Lisa and I took off for Birmingham. There are names on the Wall of guys I'd served with that brought me to tears. It was hard to look at, but a relief that an Earl Martin wasn't listed.

We looked around the exhibit. "Lisa, I shouted. "Look, there's a hooch set up just like the ones we lived in."

My legs felt weak as I walked up the wooden steps and into the dim room. That Vietnam smell filled the space. "Lisa, that's the smell I've been trying to describe. Can you smell it?"

"Yeah, I'm smelling it. It's gross."

About a month later, I was clocking out on the job site in Decatur. A guy in front of me looked familiar. Maybe from a job site somewhere. "Don't I know you?" I asked.

The guy turned around. The name Martin was printed on his hard hat. About that time he saw my name on my hard hat. I got cold chills. It was my old buddy! We yelled and hugged. Little Bit had been working construction all these years and we had finally ended up on the same project.

"It's been thirty years!" I yelled at Little Bit and anybody else who could hear our reunion.

"I've been looking all over Alabama for you. I even checked to see if your name was on the Wall," said Little Bit.

"I been looking for *you* all these years. I even went to Mississippi looking for you!"

Little Bit looked me over. "Tommy, you still walk the same and look the same, just a little grayer."

Without his hard hat, I saw that Little Bit was now bald and had put on some weight. But the good boy who'd been my buddy in Vietnam was now a grown man standing right there in front of me.

After we talked a few minutes, Little Bit hung his head. "Tommy, I'm real sorry we lost touch. But, after Vietnam, I went a little crazy, didn't do nothing right for about ten years. My first marriage broke up. I was just a mess."

That weekend we got together with my Lisa and Little Bit's sweet wife, Becky. We had a lot of catching up to do, so we rented one of those nice lake side cottages at Guntersville Lake State Park, a little bit of heaven that was thirty years and a million miles from the horror of Vietnam.

Sitting on the deck overlooking the lake, we got to talking about the miracle that Little Bit and I found each other after thirty long years. Lisa said she'd always wondered why I'd tried so hard to find my old buddy.

"I didn't know for sure, but now I think I know the answer."

Lisa took my hand as I struggled to hold back tears. Becky went over to stand behind the man she'd only known as Earl Martin, wrapping her arms around his neck. Tears streamed down his face, tears this gentle man had been holding back for thirty years.

"And what's the answer, Tommy?" asked Little Bit, a man I'd now call by his grown- up name,

"Earl Martin, I finally feel like I've got home from Vietnam."

"Peace feels real good, don't it, Tommy?"

Country Wedding

On a hot June weekend when well-heeled parents are getting their sons and daughters married off in huge downtown churches, an older couple is saying their vows in a tiny country church not far from where a ferry once crossed the Cumberland River.

Bill and Emily are marrying at a Methodist chapel where the bride's only worry is new shoes pinching her feet. The groom, age seventy, is making his third trip down the aisle.

He's been a friend for years, so I screwed up my courage, "Bill, I've been a guest at your other two weddings. Are you sure this marriage is a good idea?"

My question may have been a bit rude. And it may have been asked too late because the elderly organist was already up-front stroking the keys of the chapel's little Hammond organ. To the strains of "Blest be the Tie that Binds," Bill grinned, "You're not the first person to ask, but let me assure you that I'm absolutely confident I've got it right this time."

What a difference a few miles make. From my condo balcony overlooking one of the big city churches, I have watched catering vans grab coveted parking spots while liveried chauffeurs wait beside Rolls Royce limousines. Inside the floral wonderland of the uptown churches, wedding planners plaster smiles on their faces hoping never to have to deal with that anxious mother ever again! The uptown bride and groom are happy just to be getting this extravaganza over and done with.

Meanwhile, back at the country church, green fields surround the gravel parking lot where guests arrive in Chevrolet sedans or Ford pickup trucks. The women, dressed in their Sunday best, step cautiously across the gravel lot while carrying homemade dishes to the fellowship hall for the feast after the vows are made.

The groom made a stack cake, symbolic of his Appalachian heritage. Stack cakes, made of pancake-thin layers of cake sealed with generous slathers of apple butter between each layer, have been served at mountain weddings for generations. The bride assembled ham biscuits, another traditional food, made of homemade biscuits and slices of salty country ham.

No country wedding is complete without several platters of deviled eggs, each bearing the trademark of the maker. The bride's aunt added pickle relish to the yellow stuffing of the eggs she delivered to the fellowship hall. I saw her, hand covering her mouth, confiding to the minister's wife, "I just know my deviled eggs are much better than those pale things brought in here by the bride's best friend. Why, I bet she bought 'em at the Publix deli!"

Another must-have that the church ladies brought to Bill and Emily's wedding feast is baked beans, some made the old-fashioned way from dried beans cooked for hours in a bean pot. Others, made from canned beans 'doctored up' with mustard and barbecue sauce, are baked in the oven just long enough for the bacon topping to get crispy.

Meanwhile, what's happening over on Main Street? Wedding guests check their Rolex watches while waiting for transportation to the country club for the reception and dancing to a fourteen-piece orchestra. They've already been at the church for what felt an eternity.

Daddies write the big checks. Mothers smile modestly as they accept praise for the lovely weddings. Photographers and videographers capture every moment of the wedding and reception. Exhausted guests finally get away after spending most of the day at these glittering nuptials.

Back at the country church, the wedding took twenty minutes. Bill's grown son snapped pictures with his Canon Sure Shot. Bill's adopted daughter, a non-verbal child of a drug-addicted birth mother, beams as she squeezes between the bride and groom for the family picture. After the picture taking, Emily hugs the little girl and walks with her, hand-in-hand, to the fellowship hall. Bill strolls behind his daughter and his bride, beaming like a love-struck teenager.

Guests at the country church fill their plates with familiar foods they'll enjoy until the last deviled egg and ham biscuit are devoured. They'll share the joy of the occasion with Bill and Emily and be back home watching a baseball game on TV in just over an hour and a half. I enjoyed the food and fellowship in the church hall as much as the church regulars.

As the church ladies washed the dishes while the men took out the trash, Bill and Emily ducked out the side door and were on their way back home to East Tennessee before the sun set.

Daddy Had a Cow

Mother didn't pick the best time to break the news to Daddy that the price of milk had gone up to fifty-two cents a gallon. He was already grumpy from being left at home with four-year-old me and my brother Jim Boy, just eighteen months younger. Banging a clenched fist on the kitchen tabletop, he yelled so loudly that Jim Boy ran and hid behind our Mother.

"Damn it, that's highway robbery! Don't you dare pay that much for milk again," he roared.

Mother usually knew how to placate him, but this was not the day. "Honey," she said in her sweetest voice, "Karen and Jim Boy need milk. I need it for cooking. We can't do without it!"

"We are NOT paying fifty-two cents for any gallon of milk!" Looking from one parent to the other, I leaned against the kitchen cabinet waiting for Daddy to calm down and for Mother to throw the next punch.

She wasn't quite five feet tall, but she looked much taller when she finally got mad. "Okay, Mister, what are you going to do about it?" she questioned.

"I'll tell you what, I'm buying a milk cow," said Daddy.

"That's ridiculous," she said, stomping her foot on the linoleum floor, "We live in the Central Park neighborhood. We can't keep a milk cow in the city."

"You just watch me," he puffed.

The next day, a farm truck pulling a cattle trailer drove up the cinder-covered back alley and stopped at the garage door. I watched from my perch on the swing set as the driver jumped out of the cab and unloaded a big old Jersey cow. Daddy, with a satisfied smile, eased out of the passenger side, grabbed the rope, and led the big animal into the backyard.

I'd never seen a cow up close, but this one had a huge pink bag under her belly like a beach ball with little pink fingers attached. Mother and Jim Boy watched the scene from the back porch.

"Here's our milk wagon," said Daddy, laughing.

"Oh, my Lord!" said Mother. "What now?

So began Daddy's money-saving scheme. Just to put things into perspective, the United States was four years into World War II. Most men Daddy's age had been drafted, but he was a skilled machinist doing defense work at a Birmingham steel mill. His wages for a whole year totaled about two thousand dollars, a little more if the steel mill had a big order from the War Department that required him to work overtime.

During those war years cash money was in short supply. With rent, utilities, doctor bills and other expenses, Daddy's wages had to stretch like the waistband on a fat man's pants. It wasn't easy.

Many grocery items were rationed during the war, things like coffee, milk, sugar and meat. Mother's budget for groceries to feed a family of four was a grand total of eleven dollars a week. She worked miracles with her ration tokens when she went grocery shopping. She kept those treasured round disks in a black change purse, parting with a red one for meat and dull metal tokens for milk, sugar, coffee, and the very scarce bananas that she begged for when they weren't on the shelf.

Daddy was always amazed at how much she could buy at the store with a little cash plus her tokens. "Sweetheart, I may make the living, but you make the living worthwhile," assured a smile and a kiss from Mother.

Here's what I remember about the time the milk cow shared our yard on Court S in Central Park. Every morning, rain or shine, Daddy led the cow from her makeshift barn into what used to be our garage. The two plodded along the back alley until they reached a vacant lot, where the cow would graze all day until Daddy got home from work. Back in the garage, I watched from the doorway as Daddy milked the cow. As he milked, the big girl chomped hungrily on enough grain in the feed trough to fill the bellies of a starving army.

Every evening Daddy strode through the kitchen door, proudly swinging a bucket full of fresh milk. And most evenings, Mother praised Daddy for his effort to save those fifty-two cents a gallon for store-bought milk. "Look at this, sweetheart," she'd say, "I borrowed a churn from my sister and I'm making buttermilk and sweet creamy butter with all this good fresh milk. That's a big savings."

Meanwhile, stinking cow pies were piling up in the garage, the back alley and the vacant lot where she grazed. Daddy made a valiant effort to shovel this by-product, creating an ever-growing pile just outside the garage doors. Flies swarmed on the evil smelling refuse and the foul odor wafted through the neighborhood. At last, Daddy had to pay a farmer every week to fill his truck bed with this rotting mess and haul it away to the country.

I never knew what went wrong or why the cow disappeared. Did the City of Birmingham finally decide to enforce the livestock ordinance? Did the neighbors complain? Did the health department or the family doctor point out that young children should not be drinking raw milk? Or did the cow simply run out of milk, what the farm folks call going dry?

Daddy was a smart man. Once he got over his rage at the rising cost of milk, he did the math. First, there was the cost of the cow. Next, the cost of feed at just over a dollar for a fifty-pound bag. By the time Daddy paid the farmer to haul away the manure, he was in the hole. Not to mention the time he spent every day milking the cow and shoveling cow pies.

Every time I think of the time in my childhood when Daddy got mad and bought a cow, I recall the old saying to express shock or amazement, "Daddy had a cow when he found out in 1945 that a gallon of milk cost fifty-two cents." Daddy passed away in 2011 at the age of ninety-four. If he knew that a gallon of milk in 2024 cost just over five dollars, I think he really would have "had a cow."

Remembering the Death of a President

My family lived in a small white bungalow on Court Street in Birmingham's Central Park neighborhood when President Franklin Roosevelt died. I remember sitting on the wood plank seat in the corner of my backyard sandbox and telling my friends Jimmy Pulley and Joan Ponder that our President was dead. Jimmy was building a sandcastle, so he showed no interest in my announcement. Joan looked up from patting damp sand over her bare foot to make a tunnel that we called a frog house. "I wish you would stop saying that," she said.

I was almost five years old when the President died in Warm Springs, Georgia, on April 12, 1945. My parents were sad, so I was sad. And because I had a habit of listening when grownups talked, I heard my granddaddy say to my daddy, "Son, I wonder what will become of our country now?"

And when gravel-voiced Mrs. Hankins next door came over to visit my mother, she blew her nose and croaked, "I am completely torn up about this."

On the next day, my mother turned on the brown wooden radio in our living room and listened all day as the President's cortege was carried by train all the way from the station in Warm Springs to Union Station in Washington, DC. Every now and then, the powerful peal of church bells blared through the cloth speaker on the radio. Mother explained to me that bells rang in every city as the train rolled by. "It's a sign of respect for this great man."

During the Roosevelt era, many baby boys in the South were named Franklin or Roosevelt because the President was such a beloved figure. My own brother-in-law, born in 1942, was called Franklin until he started first grade and demanded to be called "Frank."

I can hardly believe that more than seventy-five years have passed since President Roosevelt died just three months into his fourth term as President. Many historians believe that the troubled times leading up to World War II and the war itself took a great toll on the president's health.

Of course, he had enemies as any politician does, but his enemies were few and far between in the South, where most people at the time belonged to the President's Democratic Party. Times have changed considerably since Democrats counted on the "Solid South" to win elections. President Roosevelt himself broke from his Uncle Teddy's Republican party to make a run for Congress as a Democrat. During the early 1900s, the Republican party was a liberal party that is credited with abolishing slavery and leading the country to business and commerce rather than the once dominant agrarian economy.

Despite the fact that Republicans now dominate the politics of the South, many old-timers, remembering the terrible years of the Great Depression, blamed Republican President Herbert Hoover. My father-in-law remained a staunch Roosevelt Democrat until his dying day. He was proud that his younger son carried the name Franklin. But his heartfelt feelings came through when he thought his son and I would vote for Senator Barry Goldwater in the presidential election of 1964. As the three of us argued about politics in the living room of his company-built home in the Goodyear Village of Rockmart, Georgia, he shook his head sadly. "I remember standing in bread lines during the Depression. I'll never vote for a Republican as long as I live!" And he didn't.

Dying to Get Even

My Grandpa Henry Walls lived with my family the last ten years of his life. He loved a good story, especially if he had an attentive audience. And that would be me, his youngest granddaughter, Lula.

Everybody thought Grandpa was rich, mainly because he owned land and rental houses. "Hell, I ain't rich, Lula, but it sure makes for good gossip and lots of old widder women bringing me pies and cakes."

"You better not eat those pies and cakes, Grandpa. Don't forget, you got that sugar diabetes."

"Lord 'a Mercy, honey, I don't eat none of them sweets, but I sure enjoy for the ladies to come visit. Don't you dare let on that I give their good cooking to your brothers."

Most afternoons when the weather was nice, Grandpa and I sat on the farmhouse porch. He favored a straight chair with a cane bottom while I perched on the edge of Mama's porch swing, not wanting to miss a word he said. After a while of watching the Tennessee River roll by and smelling cow pies plopped in the front pasture by Papa's cows, Grandpa looked my way. "Lula, honey, what we gonna talk about today?"

"Tell me about the Indians that lived here before the settlers came."

"I hear tell this land along the river valley was a real good hunting ground for the Injuns. Folks say this land back then was full of deer, bear, and even herds of buffaloes."

"What else, Grandpa?"

"Fish and clams was plentiful, too. You can still see rocks laid underwater in a V-shape where they built fish traps in creeks and shallow places in the river. They's still piles of clam shells around their old hunting camps. There's signs of their old camping places all around here. Me and my brothers used to find arrowheads and broken pieces of pots while we was out plowing. Used to keep our injun treasures in a cigar box."

He was wound up by now, "I can show you where an old injun school used to be. They say it was one of the first real buildings in the county besides log cabins and injun camps. White missionaries built that school. They was some of the first white people that come to this country and stayed."

"Wasn't they scared out here by themselves?"

"Them missionaries was dead set on converting the injuns. I hear they got along real good back then; that was before the natives found out that white settlers was about to take over their land. Back then, the only other white people was hunters and trappers and they was just passing through."

Next thing I know, Mama opened the screen door. "I'm just checking on you two. Daddy, do you need anything?"

Grandpa turned and smiled at Mama. "How about a dipper of water, Sarey?"

Mama came back with a dipper full of well water. She stood with us on the porch for just a minute, waving her apron tail to cool off, then headed back to the hot kitchen.

"Okay, Grandpa, what happened next?"

Waving an arm toward the river, Grandpa said he used to watch barges and steamboats pass by our farm. "When I was a boy, I seen big floats of logs headed down the river to lumber mills along the way. Some went as far as New Orleans. Floating logs was a rough life, but I heard tell there was good money in it, as long as the men and boys held on to the money long enough to get back home."

Grandpa liked to talk about the Civil War. "Lots of fightin' happened around here," he said, pointing a gnarly finger toward the ferry not far from our place.

"Was you in the war, Grandpa?"

He laughed so loud he scared the cat. "No, honey. I was just a baby during that war, but my older kinfolks told lots of tales about fightin' on Buck island. My Uncle Will told that Yankees attacked the county seat twice and burned most of the town to the ground the last time. Most of the folks around Starnesville supported the South, but up on Georgia Mountain folks went for the North so strong that they named their town for that Yankee General Grant. Didn't go over too well with the folks down here. No, ma'am, they didn't like it one bit!"

Changing subjects, I asked Grandpa how come he sold out his store and homeplace up on Georgia Mountain and come to live with us.

"I was only fifty-two years old when my Marthey died. I never cooked a meal in my life and cooking for a diabetic ain't easy. That's when my girls decided that living alone was not a good idea."

These living arrangements didn't suit Grandpa. "Some of them girls really pissed me off," he griped one afternoon out there on the porch. "One of 'em thought she could boss me around." Nodding his head in disgust, Grandpa complained that the other one "cooked the worst food I ever had the misfortune to put in my mouth."

Grandpa, I'd been told, had a knack for making money. "Before my Marthey died," he said, "we had a real nice general merchandise store in the crossroads at Bucksnort up on Georgia Mountain. Got us a little nest egg enough to buy some land up there and on the river, too."

I could tell he was right proud that he'd done well enough to own the farm my family lived on. He owned the store my papa operated. That, plus some rental houses gave him a reason to drive his horse and buggy into town to Starnesville every week or so to do his banking and catch up with the news over at the Marshall County Courthouse. Most weeks when school was out, Grandpa took me and my cousin, Marthey Elizabeth. We felt really special riding with our Grandpa, crossing the river on the ferry, then spending the dimes he gave us at the drugstore on Main Street.

I'm guessing Mama's good cooking was why Grandpa stayed with us until June of 1931, when he died at age seventy-four. I was only fourteen, but I missed him something awful.

Unfortunately, Grandpa's property and his money caused some conflict when his will was read. Those in his good graces did well. He loved my mama so she got the 500-acre farm.

Another daughter in good favor got six lots and his horse and buggy. His sons were not mentioned in the will.

Grandpa also paid for educating the two young children of his daughter Lucretia, who died when her children were babies. Both children went to college and became teachers in local schools.

Those who had earned his displeasure didn't fare too well. My papa, Walter Bayer, got a couple of acres and the store. The two daughters who pissed him off got a dollar each.

My daddy didn't complain, but the two daughters left with only a dollar bill contested Grandpa's intentions. I'll never understand why my Grandpa wrote out two of his girls. They might of rankled him, one for being bossy and the other for bad cooking; but they were his flesh and blood.

As for me, I can't put a value on the treasure Grandpa Henry left to me. Someday, I'd like to write down all those stories of the old days that he told me out there on the porch. His stories of family and history can't be bought, sold or contested. What more could I ask?

Writing Tips from Sandra Whitten Plant

Good ideas for stories or poems are fleeting,
just like money or dreams.

My first creative writing teacher, the late Lois Bell of Smyrna, Georgia, emphasized the importance of saving every idea in a folder or notebook. She said, "Write your ideas down on a napkin, scrap paper, or anything available as soon as possible. When that rainy day comes and you sit down to write, you'll never have to wonder what you were planning to write. You'll have that rich resource of ideas just waiting for you, begging to be written."

Why I Love Creative Nonfiction

Attendance at two good college journalism schools taught me how to write news stories, feature stories, and even editorials. I made a good living for thirty-four years using those basic communication skills. Imagine my happiness at retirement when creative nonfiction became a part of my writing skills palate.

What is this thing called *creative nonfiction* that I love so much? Simply put, creative nonfiction is a mostly true story that uses the techniques of fiction writing to breathe life and energy into a story. In creative nonfiction the writer is free to use the authentic voice of the speaker. That includes speech patterns, contractions, poor grammar, unsavory language, and more.

The writer is free to paint a picture of the character or characters. How does the character move, walk or talk? Characters can have a conversation that's called dialogue, almost like what you expect in a movie script. Does the story have action, conflict, or a resolution? Is there a high point to the writer's creative nonfiction story?

Now, do you see why I love creative nonfiction? In the following pages, I've included the same story written first as a narrative story and next as creative nonfiction. Which is more readable? Which is more interesting?

Narrative Story - How to get a Permanent Wave

My mother's best friend growing up was a character. Her name was Myragem Caldwell. The families lived on adjoining farms on the Tennessee River in Alabama. Mother's friend could get her granddaddy to do anything she wanted.

Mother told me about the time her friend Myragem was sitting on the front porch of the family farmhouse and crying. When her granddaddy heard Myragem crying, he came to see what was the matter.

Myragem told him she was crying because her daddy wouldn't give her three dollars so she could get a permanent in her hair. Her granddaddy gave her the three dollars and told her to get her permanent.

Creative Nonfiction - How to get a Permanent Wave

My mother's long-time friend, Myragem Caldwell, had a spark about her that made the most ordinary stories come to life. Here's one she told about how she wrapped her sweet grandpa around her little finger back when she was just a barefoot young girl on the family farm. Myragem smiled, drew a breath, and began her tale.

I was sitting on the front porch just a squalling my eyes out when my grandpa heard the racket. Grandpa came a running and sat down beside me on the porch.

"What's the matter with you, Myragem, honey? Maybe your old grandpa can help."

Still a squalling, I told him how my daddy wouldn't give me three dollars so I could get me a permanent wave.

"Is that all this is about?" asked Grandpa with a grin.

Opening up his wallet, Grandpa pulled out three dollars and handed them to me.

"You dry them tears, honey, and go get you that permanent wave."

Myragem Caldwell Conley was born on April 16, 1921, to Robert and Lee Caldwell at the family farmhouse on the Tennessee River. She lived on the farm until age seventeen when her family was relocated to make way for the waters of Guntersville Lake.

Bring your story to life. Paint pictures with words

A narrative story comes alive when the writer uses word images to paint pictures. Instead of writing that Aunt Dee flavored black-eyed peas with hog grease, try this: "A lump of fatback the size of a doorknob oozed good old hog grease to flavor the peas." (See my story "The Tricycle.")

Instead of writing that Billie Jean dragged her husband inside the door, does the following word picture show you more? "Billie Jean reached out the door to drag her tall, slim, husband Ralph inside as if he were a piece of flexible hose." (See "Love the One You're With.")

Show It, Don't Tell It!

What is meant when every creative writing teacher or editor says, "Show the action, don't just tell it?"

What works better?

Jim Boy picked up the puppy and sang to it, or Jim Boy picked up the spotted puppy, holding her up so they were face-to-face. In a tuneless croak, he sang to her, "I'm forever blowing bubbles, pret-ty bubbles in the air. They fly-eye so high..." (See "Pretty Bubbles.")

To Be a Good Writer, You Must Read, Read, Read!

The best way to learn to write is to read. Read from all genres, not just books and stories you think you may like. Look at the first line of a story. Look at the first paragraph. What did you like about the writer's style? What did you dislike? What would you change? Notice how the writer strings words together. Take special notice of word images. How many types of beginnings do you notice? Did the ending work well? Or did it look as if the writer just got tired and quit? Would you recommend the book to others?

Join a book club. Read book reviews. Be confident in your own ideas about your reading. Don't pay attention to the people who want to ban books. I am proud to have read virtually every book on the state of Florida's list of banned books. I've learned something about writing from every book I've ever read. Be proud to be a bookworm!

Find a Writing Group that's Right for You

When you find a writing group of people you trust, you are on your way to becoming a better writer. A good group is composed of people who love writing. Generous, they want to help you, and they want you to help them. A good group has ground rules such as positive or constructive comments only. A good group shares the space; no one person dominates. You and others in your trusted group often share information about writing contests, classes, workshops, or readings by noted authors; this sharing is a real benefit.

If you don't feel comfortable in a group, it's okay to leave. Writing is a lonely business. It's helpful to share space with like-minded people. But you also need that alone time to think, write, and rewrite. Always remember that your first draft usually needs work; but at least your first draft is Step One in the writing process.

Everyone Has a Story to Tell

Just think about the stories you could write. Start making a list. What about grandchildren who never heard of party-line telephones or wringer washing machines? What was downtown like when you were a youngster? Who were your childhood friends and what did you do for fun? Did you ever ride a streetcar or perhaps a passenger train to Grandma's house?

What do you recall about the days when public schools were segregated? What are your wartime memories (World War II, Korean conflict, Vietnam, Gulf Wars, Iraq, Afghanistan)? What was a momentous event in your life? What funny stories always come up when your family gets together? What is a favorite dish made by a special person in your life?

Even if you think your life is uneventful, you would be surprised at how family and friends enjoy reading those little stories from your life.

Enhance your reading experience with the help of this quick genre guide for *Sweet Adversity*. Reread, explore, and compare the diverse narratives within the collection.

Creative Nonfiction (CNF):
- Pretty Bubbles
- Sarah's Dream
- Baby Snooks
- Frozen Pane
- Open Mouth, Insert Foot
- Queen of the Road
- When Every Day was Halloween
- Baby Love
- Lula Gets the Paddle
- Papa Buys a Model A
- Baby Love
- Country Wedding
- Daddy had a Cow
- Remembering the Death of a President

Fiction Short Story (SS):
- Sweet Adversity
- Invisible
- Blue Bronco
- Love the One You're With
- Double Whammy
- Mississippi Visitation
- Winning is Everything
- Precious Memories
- Science versus Aunt Cleo
- The Tricycle
- Thirty Year War

Acknowledgments

Many thanks to best-selling author Jane Lorenzini for being a mentor and friend; To my wise and trusted friend, Billy Humphrey, author of the Wright Family Saga series; to my brother Jim Whitten, known as Jim Boy in his early years, for helping me remember highlights of our childhood. I owe a huge debt to teachers who have guided me in this writing craft, especially, the fabulous Victor Judge and dynamo Kate Myers Hansen. With much appreciation, I'd also like to thank my publisher, Jody Dyer of Crippled Beagle Publishing. To my grownup children, Jennifer Plant Johnston, and B. Andrew Plant, I'm so proud of you for your writing talent and your goodness. Much love from Mom.

About the Author

The Author attends the Appalachian Writers Workshop and visits the grave of James Still, Kentucky poet and writer, at Hindman, Kentucky.

Sandra Whitten Plant has been writing articles and stories for many years. Her favorite creative writing form is the short story, a genre that requires keen observation and economy of words. She believes that each well-written short story is like a precious jewel.

She has written articles for magazines and newspapers for many years. Her work of both fiction and nonfiction has been published in anthologies, but *Sweet Adversity* is her first book.

She has taught creative writing in schools and workshops since 1975. For the past five years, she has led a workshop called Telling Your Story in a community-based program called Joy in Learning with Westminster Presbyterian Church in Nashville, Tennessee.

Whitten Plant was born in Birmingham, Alabama, in 1941, and moved with her family to Oak Ridge, Tennessee, at the age of nine. She has studied at the University of Georgia and the University of Tennessee. She earned a B.S. degree in journalism and has done graduate work at the University of Tennessee. After a thirty-four-year-career in public and community relations, she retired in 2007 from Bechtel National, Inc. She is a resident of Nashville, Tennessee.